MW00946841

Show Up.
Step Up.
Step Out.

Leadership Through A New Lens

Neena Newberry

2013

Copyright © 2013 by Neena Newberry

All rights reserved. No part of this book may be reproduced, scanned, or distributed in any printed or electronic form without permission. Please do not participate in or encourage piracy or copyrighted material in violation of the author's rights. Purchase only authorized editions.

Contact: http://www.newberrysolutions.com

Disclaimer:
The material in this book is intended for informational and educational purposes only. No expressed or implied guarantee as to the effects of the use of the recommendations or practices can be given nor liability taken.

First Edition
First Printing, 2013

ISBN 978-1492887447

Cover Art and Design: Riot Lounge and Simmons Design Associates
Interior Book Design and Layout: Peggy Peterson

Printed by CreateSpace, an Amazon.com Company

CONTENTS

Section III - Step Out *(How Are You Using Your Leadership to Get Results and Develop Others?)*

FOREWORD

Show Up. Step Up. Step Out. Leadership Through A New Lens

I've always thought if one could "teach" common sense, he/she would be a billionaire. Accepting my aforementioned theory and having now read *Show Up. Step Up. Step Out. – Leadership Through A New Lens*, I predict that Neena will shortly become a billionaire.

Neena is a soft-spoken Servant Leader, but she has a giant Servant's Heart and a gigantic Winning Spirit that causes people to gravitate toward her for her advice and guidance regarding their personal growth/development journeys. Even a cursory review of her resume and accomplishments will tell you that she seldom disappoints these clients. She articulates her thoughts in an energetic, enthusiastic, and painstakingly simple way and she shares those same personality characteristics when she gives spot-on feedback to her clients after she has observed their "walks" versus their "talks." In addition, she is open and honest with them about what she actually "hears" as well as what she doesn't hear because she knows that each is equally important. She is quick to earn her clients' trust—not an easy task for any consultant.

Neena doesn't purport that the simple but thought-provoking nuggets offered in this book are the only way to achieve success in taking your performance and career to the next level, but I am comfortable in assuring you that if you will take the time to read and reflect upon the thoughts expressed in this enjoyable and quick read offering, you will walk away with numerous valuable common sense approaches which will produce positive results for you in your personal development and growth.

I think Neena hit a home run with this book and I hope you will enjoy looking through her "new lens" ☺.

Colleen Barrett
President Emeritus,
Southwest Airlines Co.

PREFACE

When I started writing weekly management and leadership articles, I wanted to give leaders practical advice and information that could really help them get results. From my personal experience as a leader working in demanding, high-pressure work environments, I knew that whatever I wrote had to be relevant or no one would ever read it.

Inspired by the real-world business challenges of my clients, I set out to provide thought-provoking content to help leaders take their performance and careers to the next level without taking a lot of their time. So, after almost five years of writing, I am excited to report that my readers consistently say: "I get so many articles but I always read yours. They're short enough to read quickly but they always get me thinking. And I walk away with something that I can take action on right away."

From my twenty-plus years in the corporate world, I have noticed that people may not always see the opportunities right in front of them, fully put what they know into play, or consistently focus on what *really* gets results. So, when a friend encouraged me to create a collection of my articles to serve as a valuable resource for leaders, I took it seriously. The end result is this book.

It is full of simple but thought-provoking nuggets. In less than five minutes, you can read an article and identify a strategy to help you get better results right now. Divided into three sections; Show Up, Step Up, and Step Out; this book includes ideas and easy-to-implement strategies that can make a huge difference in the short and long term.

Show Up is all about clarifying what you want others to understand about your leadership and where you can have the biggest impact on the business. Step Up focuses on uncovering blind spots, getting past roadblocks, and implementing strategies to improve your effectiveness. Finally, Step Out is about recognizing your own power and influence, building a strong network of support, and helping others step up.

This book will give you a new lens to help you see the valuable opportunities right in front of you, and simple, impactful strategies to make the most of them.

SECTION I

Show Up

(How Are You Presenting Yourself?)

THE POWER OF SIMPLY NOTICING

Most of us are so busy each day, going from one thing to the next and shifting across the many roles we play (colleagues, leaders, mentors, or parents) that in the midst of it all, we may overlook the opportunities right in front of us. So, this week, I would like you to try the exercise of "simply noticing." As you're sitting in that next meeting or conference call, pay attention to the following:

1. How You Are Showing Up

(What thoughts are running through my head?)
You may be thinking to yourself:

- "I really don't want to be here."
- "These meetings are always run poorly."
- I have way too much to do and this meeting is a waste of my time."
- "Maybe I can leave early? Will anyone care?"

(How do those thoughts affect how I am participating?)
Jot down what you're doing or not doing for that matter:

- I'm watching the clock and doodling, and am disengaged.
- I am not giving any thought to how I can really add value and move the discussion forward. I just want this to end.
- I'm planning my escape.

(What's the message I'm indirectly sending others?)
Whether you realize it or not, you are always communicating something. Sometimes it can be far from what you intend. Continuing with the scenario above, here are some potential messages you may be sending:

- My time is more important than yours.
- What you care about doesn't matter to me.
- I am not willing to roll up my sleeves and get in the game. I just want to sit on the sidelines.

2. How Others Are Showing Up

In addition to noticing what you're doing, paying attention to group dynamics can tell you volumes. To help you glean more information, ask yourself the following questions:

- Who are the informal leaders and influen·ers in this group?
- Who seems aligned with whom?
- What does each person seem to *really care about* in this discussion?
- What does the body language and energy level of each person tell you?

3. What It All Means

Now that you've had a chance to "simply notice" what's going on around you, take the time to think about what it means—even if it's just for five or ten minutes.

- What actions do you want to take as a result of your observations?
- In your next meeting, how do you want to show up instead?
- What can you do to reinforce what you want others to know about you and the value you bring?
- How can you maximize the opportunities in that next meeting, even if you do consider it a waste of your time?

This week, I challenge you to simply notice what's going on around you even if it's in just one meeting, and identify an action step you would like to take. You may be surprised at how quickly it changes your perspective. Remember that small steps can lead to big results.

INVESTING IN YOURSELF

I'd like to challenge you to think about how you're investing in your professional growth and development. When was the last time you really took the time to focus on this? Perhaps when your company asked you to fill out your goals as part of the performance management process?

Well, I want to give you a few simple ideas to consider so you can start taking action today:

1. **Put your strengths into play more powerfully.**

   Most people pay far more attention to their developmental areas than their strengths. But focusing on your strengths can give you that extra edge to take your performance to new heights. So, take a minute and jot down your top three strengths.

   When I work with my clients, I help them recognize their strengths by connecting the dots between feedback from others, what I notice in the assessments they take, and common themes that emerge in our coaching. Even if you're not working with an executive coach, you can take online assessments like the Strengths Finder or the VIA to give you additional insight and perspective.

   Once you have identified your top strengths, ask yourself, "What one or two things can I do to put these strengths into play more powerfully, in the context of my current professional goals and role in the organization?" Just asking yourself this question will help you become more intentional about using your strengths.

2. **Ask how you can be more effective.**

   Opening yourself up to feedback can be painful, but invaluable. When I conduct 360-degree interviews as part of the coaching process, I always ask the feedback providers what my client should start, stop, or keep doing to be more effective. You can do this on your own if you have the courage to put yourself "out there" and receive the input, and feel confident that people will be candid. So, think about who you would want to ask for input and how often.

   Also, remember that asking for input from others can create a solid image about your leadership style, as long as you keep your defensiveness in check. Just know that you probably will not agree with all the input, and unless you plan to do something with it, you're better off not asking for it.

3. **Think about how you want to stretch yourself.**

    Finally, as you look ahead to the next six months or a year, how do *you* want to stretch yourself? What skills or expertise do you want to further develop? What does the business really need? How will an investment in those skills or expertise enable stronger business results and advance your career?

    By getting clear about the answers to these questions you will begin to formulate a business case in your own mind about how you want to invest in yourself, and the resources you may need from your company to do so. Neither you nor your company will invest time or money if there's no ROI, so get clear about the outcomes you want to achieve.

I hope these three tips have stimulated some ideas for you. I want to challenge you to pick one area to take a small step towards this week. Remember, that small steps can lead to big results.

IS YOUR COMMUNICATION STYLE UNDERMINING YOUR CREDIBILITY?

Every day you shape how others view your leadership, through how you communicate. You send messages directly and indirectly all the time. Although this sounds really obvious, most people don't take time to think about how their communication style affects their credibility.

The biggest opportunities to improve how we communicate typically exist when we know exactly what we mean and are laser focused on our message, because this is when we may forget to provide important context. We can leave people confused or making incorrect assumptions about our intentions.

So, here are three important questions to ask yourself before you engage someone, or to have your team think through before they approach you:

1. **What do I want the other person to do with the information?**

    When you approach someone with information, the first thing they typically wonder is, "Why are you telling me this?"

    - Do you want me to take action? Help you problem-solve?
    - Are you just giving me an update?
    - Are you venting? Do you just need me to listen?

    Remember to connect the dots for others to help them understand how the information impacts them and what you expect from them.

2. **How important is this?**

    Next, ask yourself what level of priority the topic really warrants. Remember that by having a conversation focused on a single topic you may inadvertently give it more emphasis than you intended. Even the method of communication, face-to-face vs. phone or email, can convey relative importance.

    Given the level of priority (high, medium or low) what method and timing make sense? Should this topic be bundled with others? Can it wait to be discussed at a meeting you already have scheduled on another topic? Each approach communicates a different level of priority.

3. How can I connect this to the bigger picture?

Finally, consider the strategic significance of the information you want to share. If you are like most people, you have a bigger issue or business priority in mind even when you are "in the weeds." How consistently do you make that connection for others in how you frame your message?

If you are in a leader's office frequently talking about what seem like minor things at a surface level, it can undermine your credibility over time. Ensure they understand how each item relates to a bigger picture.

This week, I want to challenge you to think about these three questions as you communicate. Where do the biggest opportunities lie for you? What one step can you take to build your credibility through your communication style? Don't forget that small steps can lead to big results.

WHAT LEADERSHIP LEVERS DO YOU NEED TO PULL?

This week, I would like you to take a few minutes to assess yourself against the Ten Leadership Levers below. Each of these can dramatically impact your performance. So, take two minutes to see how you're doing.

Leadership Lever	Self-Assessment 1 (Low) – 10 (High)
1. I focus on the "right work" (the 3-4 areas that will drive the biggest results)	
2. I consistently reinforce my leadership brand	
3. I proactively manage my energy to stay productive each day and avoid burnout	
4. I clarify my intentions so others know how to interpret my actions	
5. I invest time each month to network/build stronger relationships	
6. I track my accomplishments so I can easily share them with others	
7. I tastefully toot my own horn in a way that is relevant to others and fits who I am	
8. I connect my ideas and suggestions to the bigger picture	
9. I make it easy for my advocates/sponsors to help, by sharing the information they need	
10. I communicate clearly and concisely by starting with the headlines and sharing details as needed	

As you read through the levers above, what did you notice? Remember, that this is just as much about noticing what you're doing well and putting that into play even more as it is about identifying the opportunities for improvement. I urge you to identify *one* area that you'd like to focus on and come up with an action step that you can take this week. Remember that small steps can lead to big results.

DO YOU KNOW WHAT REALLY DIFFERENTIATES YOU?

As I have coached high performing leaders over the years, I can't help but notice some common themes. As they move up the ladder, sometimes they take for granted how hard it would be for someone to fill their shoes. Or they underestimate the value of their perspective, one that has been shaped by a unique set of personal and professional experiences.

So, today, I want to ask, "When is the last time you stopped to think about what makes you truly unique and valuable to an organization, whether it's your current employer, a client or prospect?" If you're like most people, you spend little to no time contemplating what differentiates you—unless you're actively job hunting or lobbying for a pay increase or promotion. Yet going through this process can help you step up your game, leveraging your unique value in a way that serves you and your company.

To clarify what sets you apart, start by answering the three questions below. Remember that this won't take the place of a more thorough personal leadership branding exercise, but it will get the ball rolling in the right direction.

1. **What common themes do you see in the type of work others ask you to do?**

    Sometimes it takes other people repeatedly pulling you into certain types of projects or opportunities before you notice that what you bring to the table is unique *and* valued. Think about some of your experiences over the past six to nine months. What jumps out at you?

2. **What have you heard others say about your work?**

    What do others value most about your work? I want you to think about it from two vantage points, what you do *and* how you do it. Also consider what you have heard people consistently say, whether or not their feedback made it into your performance review.

3. **What skills or perspective do you have that would be hard to replace?**

    Finally, get to the aspects that cannot be easily replicated, i.e., your unique approach, perspective, skills, or background. People often openly point these out when they initially meet or get to know you. So, think about conversations you have had with people who have known you for little time, as well as those who have known you for years. What have you heard them say?

It may help to start by asking a few people you trust for input. But even if you don't, you should gain some insight from answering the questions yourself. If you want to take the exercise one step further, identify one small step to highlight or leverage your unique value, in the context of your career goals and what's important to business.

WHAT IS YOUR RISK TAKING PROFILE?

I recently had a conversation with one of my female executive clients about the topic of risk taking as a leadership competency. I would venture to say that most of you probably don't sit around contemplating whether or not you are a risk taker and what that really means, especially if risk taking comes naturally to you. As I helped her think through her upcoming presentation on the topic, we discussed a few ideas you may appreciate.

Many of us have negative thoughts when we think about risk. But at its core, what is risk management all about? Some might say it's all about minimizing losses. But my client, whose role centers around risk management for her company, explained that *risk is all about uncertainty—in the context of value protection and value creation.* In other words, as you contemplate whether or not to take a risk, you weigh the potential loss against the potential gain. *Either way, you consider what is at stake, and it impacts how you "show up" and how others view your leadership.*

To give you more insight about your appetite for risk taking, take a look at the scenarios below and notice how many of these would be true for you:

✓ I confidently voice my opinion even when I know it is counter to what others think

✓ I would raise my hand for that stretch role or assignment knowing I haven't mastered all the requisite skills

✓ I willingly ask for what I want and need—like that promotion, pay increase, or developmental opportunity

✓ When there aren't enough seats at the boardroom table for everyone, I would take the one at table instead of the one against the wall

If risk taking makes you uncomfortable, here are four targeted strategies that can help you push the envelope a little more:

1. **Gather data.**

   Relevant information can help you weigh the pros and cons of a particular situation and make more rational versus emotional decisions.

2. **Build personal capital.**

   Invest in developing your leadership brand. It can help others correctly link your actions with your intent, so when you do go out on a limb it's not as risky.

3. **Create a strong network.**

   Surround yourself with people who will challenge your perspective, ideas, and ways of thinking. Their influence may lead you down a different path than you might have otherwise chosen. Also, be sure to consider individuals with influence and power, so they can help you mitigate personal risk.

4. **Visualize success.**

   Let yourself imagine what it would mean to you and for the company if you achieved the goal for which you are taking risks. How would it feel? What might happen?

Whether or not you view yourself as a risk taker, hopefully your wheels are now turning about how you can integrate more risk taking as part of your leadership style and approach. I want to challenge you to come up with one action you can take this week to push yourself beyond your comfort zone, and use one of the strategies above to help you. You never know where it might lead.

HOW TO DISAGREE WITHOUT
BEING DISAGREEABLE

During an interesting lunch conversation with a successful female business leader here in Dallas, we discussed how difficult it can be for some women to voice a difference of opinion in a way that will be well-received (i.e., not too assertive).

On the other hand, saying nothing can have negative consequences of its own (i.e., being viewed as not assertive enough). So, if you've found yourself waffling back and forth about whether to speak up or bite your tongue, read on.

1. **Don't be a derailer.**

   I want you to think back to a time when you sat in a meeting thinking to yourself, "I don't agree with the direction we are heading in" and then you didn't say a word. Perhaps you thought it was the wrong forum in which to voice your concerns.

   What was the impact of your choice? Did you catch people off guard by not speaking up in that moment and later sharing privately that you had major concerns? Regardless of your intent, how were you viewed? Did some think you were being passive-aggressive or maybe not assertive enough? Did others wonder, "Why didn't she just say something when we were all there? It could have saved us a lot of time." Also recognize that others may have unvoiced concerns, so by speaking up you might just give them the courage to share them.

   Finally, remember that you can express a different point of view in the moment without turning it into a big deal. For example, if your concerns will warrant a lot more discussion, you can suggest an offline discussion with a smaller group if that makes sense. The next two strategies below might also help.

2. **Frame your disagreement as "Yes and . . ."**

   Before you highlight points of concern, acknowledge areas of alignment. By first demonstrating that you "get it" (i.e., that you understand the other person's point of view and what could work well) others will be more open to your perspective.

Some people fall into the trap of jumping straight into what they think won't work, which can trigger defensiveness—and then they entirely forget to point out what they *do* like about the idea. So, challenge yourself to say, "Yes and ..." instead of "No, but ..."

3. **Depersonalize your comments.**

   Finally, remember to keep it objective by evaluating each idea against the intended outcomes. In other words, point out the criteria for success (stated or implied) and help others understand how the ideas on the table do or don't satisfy them. This makes the evaluation of the ideas feel much less personal, and the originator of the idea is less likely to feel attacked when you give your feedback. By framing your suggestions in the context of the group's objectives, others will be more receptive to what you have to say.

Sometimes saving your disagreement for another time is indeed the best option. But in many cases, it may not be. My goal here is to challenge you to be more assertive in expressing your views while considering the impact on how you're viewed as a leader. So, before you move on with your day, take a minute to identify one step you'll take to put these ideas into play this week.

IS SELF-CARE REALLY SELFISH?

I have to give my sister credit for inspiring this article. She just wrote a book on successful working women, the challenges they face in making marriage work, and how to overcome them. As we talked about common themes that we see in our respective worlds working with high performing women, we talked about the difficulty women have with the concept of self-care.

We discussed that women often confuse self-care with selfishness. A woman may think, "How could I possibly take time for *me* right now when there's so much to do and others rely on me?" In this view of the world, self-care is a luxury, a "nice-to-have."

A man, on the other hand, knows that self-care allows him to keep going so he *can* provide the support others need from him. In this view of the world, self-care is a "must have" that provides energy. That doesn't mean a man will put himself first no matter what. However, he is much less likely to confuse self-care with selfishness.

At the end of the day, what we're talking about is energy management. Resist the temptation to keep giving and giving without taking enough time to renew your own energy. As you may know from firsthand experience, it can lead to burnout or resentment pretty quickly.

So, I want you to think about what you will do for yourself this week, to give yourself that essential energy you need to stay productive and avoid burnout. Here are some ideas that came from a group of executive women at the Greater Houston Partnership and a group I facilitate at Shell.

1. **Say no to something you really don't want to do.**

    Whether it's a personal or professional request, resist the temptation to say yes to something you don't want to do—and know you shouldn't be doing. If you feel guilty about saying no, you can always help the person find another resource to help. Remember that this task could be a good developmental opportunity or exposure for someone else.

2. **Get exercise without putting any judgment around it.**

   You might just have 15 minutes to exercise so adopt the mindset that 15 minutes is better than nothing. If exercise gives you energy, make the most of whatever time you have by taking a quick walk, going for a short run, grabbing some dumbbells, or doing a few pushups and sit-ups.

3. **Give yourself time to decompress before you walk into the house.**

   Take time to transition out of work mode, so you can leave work stress at the office. Do something to deliberately make that shift, whether you sit in the car for a few minutes to get the solitude you need before you immerse yourself into a house full of children, or just don't take that conference call on the drive home.

If you are someone who regularly put everyone else's needs ahead of your own, identify one step you will take this week to take care of yourself—so you *can* be there for others. Remember that self-care isn't selfish.

HOW ARE YOU GETTING IN YOUR OWN WAY?

When you're a high performer, you may have a relentless drive for results. Your expectations of yourself may be much higher than what others expect of you and failure is usually not an option. Although you have a remarkable ability to get results, you may fall into some traps that limit your effectiveness. Read through the traps below to see if any apply to you.

1. **I mind read.**

   If you frequently interrupt others because you know what they are going to say, I urge you to simply notice the impact your behavior has on them. Pay attention to how they react including their body language, tone of voice, actions, and words. What do all those things tell you? I would guess that you are sending them some messages you had not intended to: "What you have to say doesn't matter." "My opinion carries more weight than yours." "I don't have time to listen to your input."

2. **I always know the right answer.**

   If you fall into this trap, you may have a high aptitude and can come up with the right answer most of the time (and usually much faster than others). So, you may not see a strong need to solicit input from others or explain the assumptions and facts behind your recommendations or solutions.

   Although you may have the "right" answer, ask yourself what will maximize your effectiveness as a leader. How much of it is about getting to the absolute best solution, even if others won't implement it? How much of it is about getting to a workable solution that others can support?

   It often helps to go back and think about what happened the last time you pushed really hard for what you thought was the right answer. Remember that how you share your ideas is just as if not more important than the idea itself—and that you can do it in a way that engages others and leverages your expertise.

3. **I set the bar very high.**

   Having high expectations of yourself and others can bring value as long as you do it in a way that still motivates and energizes others. Remember that not everyone views their careers in the same way you do. Some may see it as a source of security rather than a source of fulfillment. By understanding what motivates each of your team members, you will have valuable information that will help you develop an effective approach and minimize your frustration.

4. **I take over when others don't do things the way I would.**

   Micromanaging is a common trap that can completely distract you from making the highest and best use of your talent and skills. Remember to ask yourself what you're giving up when you say "yes" to spending time creating a perfect deliverable when someone else could have done it well (just not as perfectly as you). Did it mean you had to work later to get to the higher priority work you should have been doing instead? Did it mean you couldn't exercise or spend as much time with your family?

If you fall into one more of these traps, remember that we all do things that get in our own way. I urge you to identify one small step you will take this week to make a change in the right direction to avoid falling into the same trap again. And be sure to tell someone else about it so they can encourage you and assess your progress.

WHAT KIND OF LEADER ARE YOU?

When was the last time you really thought about your brand as a leader? If you're like most people, you probably haven't given it much, if any, thought. When I coach high performing managers and leaders, leadership brand comes up time and again—because being deliberate about assessing and developing your brand can have a huge impact on your success.

So, if you're ready to take a look at your brand, here are four steps to get you started:

1. **Find out what you are known for today.**

   Whether you realize it or not, you do have a brand. The question is, "How well is it serving you as a leader?" As you define your current brand, limit yourself to three one-word adjectives. Reflect on performance reviews and common themes you have heard from others in the past, and consider collecting feedback from others. You can conduct an anonymous online survey, ask people yourself, or have someone else (like an executive coach, mentor, or supervisor) gather feedback for you.

   Whatever you do, choose an approach that will give you candid information. *Remember to ask people to give you specific examples. What do you say or do that demonstrates your brand? You have to understand what it looks and sounds like.*

2. **Determine what you want to be known for.**

   Your desired brand must be authentic (i.e., true to you); this not about misleading anyone. Again, limit yourself to three one-word adjectives. Just earlier this week, I coached a female executive (let's call her Michelle) about her desired brand.

   She wants others to view her as:

   Credible – Michelle wants others to recognize her specialized industry expertise because it is important for the role and business she is in.

   Confident – Michelle wants to have a physical presence that conveys that she is a strong player.

Respectful – When she disagrees with a point of view, Michelle wants to do it in a manner that still encourages ideas and input from others.

3. **Define how to reinforce your desired brand.**

   Again, it's important to determine what you would say or do to reinforce your brand. In Michelle's example, demonstrating credibility might involve proactively sharing specific industry information with the leadership team in the context of a high priority or project. Confidence might entail speaking louder, making direct eye contact when addressing a group, standing or sitting taller, or speaking up at least once in every leadership meeting.

4. **Take action to close the gap.**

   Identify 1-2 actions you will take to close the gap between your current and your desired brand. *This may mean that you have to stop or start doing something.* Using Michelle's example of being respectful, she has to stop interrupting others when they speak and resist that urge to jump right in.

Just remember that your leadership brand is important context for how you show up as a leader—in your everyday words and actions. By proactively defining and managing your brand, you will get better results. So, what are you waiting for?

MAKING CHANGE STICK

When my son learned to tie his shoelaces, I distinctly recall that intense look on his face as he focused so hard on each step in the process to make sure he did it all just right.

I'm sure you haven't had to put that level of energy and focus into tying your shoes in years because you have reached that point of unconscious competence (where it's second nature). However, you may have other things you want to master or change to take your leadership and performance to the next level.

When I coach leaders, my goal is to help them make the desired changes, and make them stick. As you might expect, there is a method to the madness. So, today, I want to share three tips that may expedite the change process for you.

1. **Remind yourself what's at stake.**

   Usually when you want to make a change in behavior, it's because something much bigger is at stake. Let me explain what I mean. For example, I recently coached a client who is so smart that he often goes into mindreading mode. In other words, he keeps interrupting others because he "knows" what they are about to say.

   He has finally come to realize the negative impact that this has on his relationships and wants to make a shift. At the end of the day, this isn't about him wanting to be more polite and waiting patiently for others to finish. As a leader, this is about him building commitment by showing respect and valuing his team's ideas. And for the business, it's about delivering on the business goals as efficiently and effectively as possible. By keeping in mind what's really at stake, he is much more motivated to follow through.

2. **Recognize that others won't notice immediately.**

   As you put in the time and effort to change your behavior, you might feel frustrated when others just don't seem to notice. Remember that with the day-to-day distractions in their lives, most people will take a while to notice. And when they do, it may take time for them to trust that you can sustain the behavior change—

and that has less to do with you and more to do with human nature.

3. **Set aside time to assess your progress.**

    Last but not least, take time to understand what's working for you and what's not. By deliberately looking for the evidence, you will notice what's working and will think about how to more proactively put it into play. Although change takes time, this approach will make change stick much faster.

So, whether you are making change on a small or large scale, identify one strategy you want to put into play for yourself this week. What small step will you take to make change stick?

PUT MORE POWER INTO YOUR COMMUNICATION STYLE

I had the opportunity to hear author Connie Glaser speak at a Network of Executive Women event about how women undermine their own power in how they communicate. I see this time and again with my coaching clients, and I have made some of these mistakes myself.

Women often don't realize how their communication style gets in their way or impacts how others view their leadership. Although women may have good intentions, those may not be apparent in their communication. I think this quote drives the point home: *"We judge ourselves by our intent, but we judge others by their actions."* So, remember that your actions may be doing you a disservice, no matter how positive your intentions.

Let's take a look at three common communication traps to see if any of them apply to you.

1. **Getting into the Weeds**

   Women often make the mistake of building up to their conclusions, rather than starting with the two or three key headlines. They often don't realize how this can diminish their credibility. By taking everyone through the details first, they run the risk of losing their audience in a sea of information, or giving the impression that they can't see the big picture or get out of the weeds. Remember you can always provide additional information if others need it—so *lead with the headlines*.

2. **Holding Back**

   Have you ever been in a meeting and never said a word? Perhaps it's because you agreed with what others said and you didn't see a need to convey that. Or maybe you didn't want to be rude and talk over someone to get your point across. Or perhaps, you simply wanted to respect everyone else's time and not prolong an already long meeting. Whatever your rationale, what did your participation (or lack thereof) convey to others? Did your presence really make a difference?

So next time, speak up! Before you walk into that meeting or jump on that conference call, take five minutes to anticipate what will be discussed and develop your point of view. This will make it easier to dive right in, contribute to the discussion, and get your voice heard.

3. Treading Too Softly

Women sometimes use a tone of voice or language that reduces their power and influence. Their voice may take on a higher pitch at the end of a sentence, giving the impression that they're asking a question rather than making a statement with a strong sense of conviction. They may speak too quietly, or use words that communicate indecisiveness: "I think"; "I guess"; and so on."

So, pay attention to what you say and how you say it. To get a better sense of how your communication comes across, ask people you trust for feedback so you know what to watch for.

The good news is that you can address these issues through minor tweaks in your communication. So, before you move on to your busy day, identify one small step you will take this week to put more power into your communication style. Remember that small steps can lead to big results.

PRESENTATION PEARLS OF WISDOM

I attended a panel discussion at the Greater Houston Women's Conference with three professionals who collectively have over 75 years of experience in acting, radio and TV. They shared some valuable reminders and tips about Presenting Your Best Self On and Off Camera. So, I've included four things to think about the next time you're preparing to be in front of an audience:

1. **Who is my audience and what will they want from me?**

   Any presentation starts with thinking about your audience. Even if your audience is just one person, first take a few minutes to put yourself in their shoes. Think about what they will want from you whether it's information, reassurance, or something else. This will go a long way in helping you position your ideas in a way that addresses *their* underlying needs and resonates with them.

2. **What do I want from my audience?**

   As a presenter, you also typically want something from your audience. For example, you may want them to feel confident in your abilities or think you are the right person for the job. Knowing what you want from your audience will give you more insight into the type of information to present and *how* to best communicate it.

3. **What is my story?**

   Remember that storytelling is powerful—and there's *always* a story line. A talented Deloitte partner taught me this lesson early on in my career. To this day, I remember walking into his office with a draft presentation for a client meeting. He left it sitting untouched on his desk until he asked me a series of questions. I can't remember the exact questions but they led me to give him the 3-4 headlines, the key messages we really needed our client to know and understand.

   By the time we finished talking, I knew I had missed the mark with my presentation. I had a gold mine of information (supporting charts, data, etc.) but I hadn't effectively woven it into a compelling story that made the "so what" crystal clear. I remember sheepishly reaching across his desk to take back my work, hoping he wouldn't look at it first.

4. What do I need to do to take my nerves out of the equation?

The last two tips focus on addressing nervousness that many of us experience when it comes to presenting in front of an audience, especially when a lot is at stake. Nervousness can come from not being fully aligned or associated with your story, or focusing more on yourself than your audience.

On the first issue, the best advice I can give you is to practice saying your presentation out loud. According to the panelists, three times is the magic number to imprint the script in your memory. Think about how valuable this preparation could be if a meeting runs over and your presentation time gets drastically shortened. Knowing your story would help you quickly distill your presentation down to the essential headlines.

Second, remember to focus on your audience instead of yourself. Many of us can't help but zero in on our own fears and what others think of us. So, to address this, imagine that your audience is full of people that you enjoy being around, and that your primary objective is to serve them. By staying focused on what your audience needs you will focus less on your fears.

After reading through this, I hope you realize that there are some small steps you can take to prepare that can make a big difference in the effectiveness of your presentations. Remember that taking even as little as five minutes to think through these questions can go a long way. So, I would urge you to identify one practice that you'd like to start incorporating today.

DO YOU PROVIDE "STRATEGIC SNAPSHOTS" OF YOUR PERFORMANCE?

If you're like most people, you have a sense of what you want to accomplish when each day begins—and then the day "happens." You may get diverted by unplanned issues and be left wondering, "What the heck happened?!"

No matter what is going on in your day, I urge you to think about the countless opportunities you have to showcase what you're doing to add value and make a difference. I like to call this providing "strategic snapshots" of your performance. In my signature presentation "Getting the Visibility You Want" (aka, "Tastefully Tooting Your Own Horn") and in my coaching, I offer a range of strategies on how to do this in a way that works for you.

Before I dive into giving you my tips, I want you to consider the following points as important context.

- **We are all busy—usually too busy to notice how others are adding value and contributing on a day-to-day basis.**

  It's not that we don't want to notice; it's just that our attention is divided. And your boss is probably no different from you in this respect. So, *you* have to help your boss notice how you're making a difference. I'd like to say a mid-year or year-end discussion as part of your formal performance management process is enough—but it just isn't. When I led Performance Management & Career Planning at Deloitte, I came to fully appreciate how often people are out of synch with their boss's view of their performance.

- **This isn't about bragging.**

  At the end of the day, this is about sharing important information that can add value to your company and shape the direction of your career. Remember that as someone who has a personal stake in your performance and development, your boss needs to know how and what you're doing. And others in the company can benefit from learning about how you overcame specific challenges and what led to your success.

  Here are three suggestions on how to provide "strategic snapshots" of your performance:

1. **Be clear about what you want to be known for.**

    Your desired brand/reputation serves as important context and a filter for what to share with others. So, take the time to get clear about the 2-3 things you want people to think of when they think of you. This isn't about trying to be someone you're not. It's about helping others understand what differentiates you and why that matters.

2. **Notice the opportunities in front of you.**

    Before you go into a meeting, have a call with someone, or write an email, ask yourself, "How can I demonstrate how I'm adding value, or reinforce my desired brand in this interaction?" Every interaction may not afford this opportunity, but asking yourself this question will lead you to provide "strategic snapshots" of your performance more often.

3. **Find an approach that fits your style.**

    As you know, some people have no problem telling others how they are adding value while others struggle because they don't want to come across as arrogant, or self-promotion doesn't fit with their cultural norms. So, don't just adopt someone else's approach. Take the time to think about what fits your personal style.

    As a first step, think about a couple of accomplishments you'd like to share and how and why they have relevance and value to others. By going through this thought process you will present the information differently—less like bragging and more like information that others really need to know.

Remember that it's up to you to consistently share and reinforce what you want others to know about your contributions (i.e., provide "strategic snapshots" of your performance) no matter how your day unfolds. And it doesn't have to involve a huge effort or time commitment. You should know my mantra by now: "Small steps can lead to big results."

WHAT'S GETTING IN THE WAY OF YOUR SUCCESS?

I specialize in working with high performing managers and leaders (especially women) to help them get even better results. So, the people I work with are typically very talented, have done well in their careers, and are striving for more.

As they move up the corporate ladder, the skills they need to be successful are much less about their technical knowledge and much more about their ability to work with and through others—which really gets to the heart of interpersonal and leadership skills.

Marshall Goldsmith, a well-known executive coach and author of the book *What Got You Here Won't Get You There* compiled a list of common habits that limit an individual's success. Take a minute to read through this and put a check mark next to any that apply to you.

1. **Winning too much:** The need to win at all costs
2. **Adding too much value:** The overwhelming desire to add your two cents to every discussion
3. **Passing judgment:** The need to rate others and impose your standards on them
4. **Making destructive comments:** The needless sarcasms and cutting remarks that we think make us sound sharp and witty
5. **Starting with "No," "But," or "However":** The overuse of these negative qualifiers which secretly says to everyone, "I'm right. You're wrong."
6. **Telling the world how smart we are:** The need to show people we're smarter than they think we are
7. **Speaking when angry:** Using emotional volatility as a management tool
8. **Negativity, or "Let me explain why that won't work.":** The need to share our negative thoughts even when we weren't asked
9. **Withholding information:** The refusal to share information in order to maintain an advantage over others
10. **Failing to give proper recognition:** The inability to praise and reward
11. **Claiming credit that we don't deserve:** The most annoying way to overestimate our contribution to any success

12. **Making excuses:** The need to reposition our annoying behavior as a permanent fixture so people excuse us for it
13. **Clinging to the past:** The need to deflect blame from ourselves and onto events and people from our past; a subset of blaming everyone else
14. **Playing favorites:** Failing to see that we are treating someone unfairly
15. **Refusing to express regret:** The inability to take responsibility for our actions, admit we're wrong, or recognize how our actions affect others
16. **Not listening:** The most passive-aggressive form of disrespect for colleagues
17. **Failing to express gratitude:** The most basic form of bad manners
18. **Punishing the messenger:** The misguided need to attack the innocent who are usually only trying to help us
19. **Passing the buck:** The need to blame everyone but ourselves
20. **An excessive need to be "me":** Exalting our faults as virtues simply because they're who we are

As Marshall says in his book, the good news is that it's hard to find successful people who embody too many of these. Usually, a person is guilty of one or two of them. *Even if you put a check mark next to six or eight of these habits, all of them may not be significant enough to worry about. So, distill your list down to one or two key things to start with.*

The other exciting part is that these issues can be simple to correct because you already have the skills to do so. For example, I have a client who had difficulty being fully present and listening to others (#16) in meetings because she was constantly distracted by her BlackBerry. So, she came up with a simple solution, to put her BlackBerry away during meetings. Another client noticed that he failed to give proper recognition, and decided to carve out 15-20 minutes each Friday to send emails or notes to 1-2 of his staff to acknowledge their contributions.

Remember that we all have habits that get in the way of our success. To start, just focus on two that will make the biggest difference to your effectiveness as a leader, and identify and implement 1-2 small steps you can take to address them.

ARE YOUR HEADLINES GETTING LOST IN THE DETAILS?

No matter how high up you go in an organization, communication can be a challenge. As a manager or leader, there's a fine line between sharing too much information and not enough. Too much detail can leave others with the impression that you can't see the big picture or focus on what really matters, because you are bogged down in minutia. Or people may think you are defensive when you dive into details in response to a question or comment, even if your intent is to merely explain or inform. On the other hand, not sharing enough detail may leave others thinking that you don't fully understand the situation or issues at hand.

Wherever you are on the scale of detail-orientation, the most important thing is to make sure that the person receiving your communication gets the "headlines," the 2-3 key messages you really want them to understand.

Here are some guidelines I use with my executive coaching clients to help them focus on what to say and how to say it.

1. **Consider the kind of impression you want to leave, and how you want to be viewed.**

    Taking this into consideration will help you determine the best method(s) to use for your communication (e.g., call, email, meeting, etc.), how to frame your message, and how you "show up." Remember that how you communicate can reinforce or detract from the leadership brand you want to build.

2. **Map out the 2-3 key messages that you want your audience to leave with.**

    If you had only 60 seconds to get your message across, what are the most critical things you want your audience to know? Once you've figured that out, think about how you can make those messages stand out, and connect your supporting information back to them. For example, if you are putting it in writing, using color and bold can help. If you are presenting the information in a group or one-on-one, you can use your handouts/material to reinforce your key messages.

3. **Practice sharing your headlines first then filling in the details to ensure understanding.**

    Sometimes we can fall into the trap of providing all the information to support our point of view, and then conclude with our summary of what it all means. Most leaders expect that you have done your homework—especially if you are high performer—and will ask you for more information if they need it. So, if you assume they want all the detail, you may lose their attention. Of course there are some leaders who are very detail-oriented, so adjust your style for your audience.

    Either way, I would encourage you to start with the headlines and then provide more information as needed. This would work whether you are communicating something for the first time or merely responding to someone else.

Often, *minor tweaks in your communication can make a huge difference.* Just make sure you aren't losing your audience in all the detail.

HOW ARE YOUR BLIND SPOTS GETTING IN YOUR WAY?

Blind spots. We all have them. But do you really understand how they're getting in the way of your success?

Let me give you an example to bring this to life. Imagine racing a high performance car. You are looking ahead, planning your next move to sustain your performance without compromising your speed. You need to switch lanes and have just a split second to make a decision about which way to go. But you can't see because your car has a huge blind spot. What do you do? Do you slow down and risk losing the race? Or do you move to the next lane, with unknown consequences to you and others?

Like a race car driver, a high performing leader moves at a fast clip—zipping from one move to the next, making quick decisions; all the while focused on getting results. If you are like many leaders, you have limited time to reflect. So, you may not realize that you have *blind spots—behaviors that could be hindering your progress and possibly putting others at risk.*

So, what can you do? Here are three tips to help you identify and address your blind spots:

1. **Ask others for feedback.**

   Identify people with a range of perspectives, who will be open and honest about your performance, and ask them for feedback. Be sure to ask what you do well, how you may be getting in your own way, and what you should do more or less of to be effective in your role.

   As you prepare to request feedback, think about the importance of anonymity and the approach that will yield the most insight. For example, you can use your company's 360 or upward feedback tool, use a simple online survey tool like Survey Monkey, sit down and have a direct conversation, or work with an executive coach who can interview others on your behalf and summarize the key themes. *Whatever you decide, be sure to choose a method that fosters honest, candid feedback and gives you enough context to interpret the comment.*

2. **Validate the feedback.**

    Everyone reacts to feedback differently. You may find yourself choosing to deny it or ignore it. However you feel about the feedback, I would urge you to at least validate it. Look for evidence and examples through your own observations, reflection and conversations with others. Whether you agree with the feedback or not, entertaining the possibility that "it might be true" will open you up to noticing things you might not otherwise see— yes, "seeing" the blind spots.

3. **Take action.**

    So now that you have gathered and validated the feedback, what should you do? Just remember that feedback only has value if you do something with it. Start by choosing one or two areas that you'd like to focus on first. Be careful not to overload yourself with action items, and remember that your action items don't have to be huge. Small steps can lead to big results.

Revealing your blind spots can be a powerful way to take your performance to the next level, so take the time to figure out what they are. It will be well worth the investment.

TACKLING IMPORTANT ISSUES HEAD ON

Have you ever been so overwhelmed by an issue that it's hard for you to take any action, even when you *know* you need to? Maybe all you can think about is the time and energy it will take to think through the problem, and the implications of the possible outcomes. Well, you're not alone. The good news is that there are some practical ways to get "unstuck" and move forward. The best way I can illustrate this is by describing a recent coaching conversation.

Jane and I discussed her need for more flexibility in her work hours and location. She feels compelled to make a change because she just isn't happy. Jane has worked very hard to get to her current level of career success and is valued by her company, but she is afraid to rock the boat. She loves her work and isn't ready to give up a good thing, but she is also exhausted by her hectic schedule between work and home.

She feels like her only options are to live with it or leave her job. As you can imagine, the thought of leaving her job scares her. What if she can't replicate what she values about her current role and employer or, even worse, what if she can't find a job at all in the current economy?

So, you can see how a situation like this could be overwhelming. The bottom line is that she feels stuck and hasn't taken any action.

Regardless of the specific situation, here are three key things to consider when tackling an issue:

1. **Examine how you've framed the issue.**

   It's important to ask yourself a few questions to make sure you've framed the issue appropriately: "What problem am I really trying to solve? How else can I look at the situation? How narrowly have I defined the issue?" In Jane's case, her focus was on choosing whether to live with her current situation or leave her job. But at the heart of it, it was really more about getting the flexibility she needed in her life—not just choosing between two options. Once she reframed the issue, she could envision options that felt more comfortable than the two in front of her.

2. **Identify what is really keeping you from taking action.**

    In Jane's situation, one important factor is that she is exhausted and doesn't have the energy or time to reflect—which is what she said she needs to make a good decision. So, rather than jumping right in to solve the bigger issue ("live with it" or "leave it"), she needs time to get some perspective. For Jane, the options could range from setting some boundaries for work, taking vacation time, taking a leave of absence, or asking others for help.

3. **Break the bigger issue down into manageable pieces.**

    Ask yourself, "What do I need to take action on right now? Is it really solving the entire problem?" Maybe all you need to do is figure out where to start. If you can commit to one or two small steps in the right direction, often that's enough to create the momentum you need to keep going.

    In Jane's case, she needs to define her flexibility needs. What would that mean in terms of hours and work schedule? How would that impact her ability to get her job done? What support would she need from the company? At the end of the day, what is she really asking for?

So if you are tackling an important issue (whether it's about flexibility or something else) and feel stuck, take a deep breath and ask yourself a few questions. It can do wonders to help you move forward. How you frame a problem and break it down can make a huge difference in your ability to solve it. Just remember to also work through any underlying issues that may be holding you back.

So, at this point you might be wondering, "How does Jane's story end?" Well it's still in process, but I'm happy to report that she is exploring some creative win/win options with her current employer.

SECTION II

Step Up

(How Are You Taking Your Leadership Up a Notch?)

STAYING FOCUSED ON THE BIG PICTURE

As managers and leaders, you may have a wide range of responsibilities from giving your team the right guidance and direction to getting down into details to problem-solve. However, the higher you climb up the corporate ladder, the more you need to consistently focus on the big picture in everything you do. This can make a huge difference in whether others perceive you as a leader, and in your ability to get results.

When I work with my clients, one of the first things I ask them to do is identify the three areas where they can make the biggest impact on the business. Then I take it one step further and have them identify what makes each of those three things so important, to the business and to them personally (e.g., to their goals and development as leaders).

This approach is a core part of my Leadership System because it helps people focus on the big picture *and* recognize the "so what." In other words, identifying where you need to redirect your focus is an important first step—but understanding the impact of that shift will cement your commitment to doing it and help you articulate it to others.

By asking the two questions above early on, I find that most people quickly zero in on the 20 percent of their activity and effort that matters the most. It gives them a new lens to look at things through. So, they begin to challenge how they spend their time and start to recognize what they should stop doing altogether. This process of rationalizing their time and focus opens up new possibilities, including delegating to and developing others who are eager to show what they can do.

However, to really be viewed as a strong leader by others you have to go beyond redirecting how you spend your time. You also have to help others "see" that you are doing so. In other words, make your big picture more visible to other leaders, your boss, peers, and staff through what you communicate.

Sometimes we can be so clear in our own heads about what we are doing that we can forget that our underlying intent and actions may not be well understood by others. So, look for opportunities, big and small, to communicate your big picture and priorities to others—the "what" and the "why." And you don't have to create new forums to do so; you can leverage existing meetings and opportunities. Whatever approach you choose, be sure to tailor it to your audience.

Finally, remember that your communications and actions must be in sync because your actions will speak louder than your words. For example, if people see you consistently focused on the details in meetings and in their interactions with you, it will be much more difficult for them to view you as someone who sees and understands the big picture.

So, I'll end with a Call to Action. Please take the time to answer the following questions for yourself today:

- What are the three things you need to focus on in the next six months, to have the biggest impact on the business and on your own development?
- What makes each of these things so important to you and the business (i.e., what will the impact be)?
- What one step will you take to communicate your big picture to others?

These questions will help you focus on the big picture—on what really drives value and results. So, keep them handy and review them every six months.

CREATING THE OUTCOME YOU WANT

My sweet spot is working with high performers—especially women. For those of you wondering, I do actually work with some pretty impressive men too. Regardless of gender, what I find in this group of clients is a relentless drive for results. But even with that drive, sometimes people overlook how they can create the outcomes they want.

For example, I met with a leader who was excited about a promising business relationship that could really take his company to the next level. After having two fruitful meetings with this potential client, he shifted into "wait and see" mode because he felt the ball was in the other party's court.

Although he may not have had as much control as he wanted in this situation, he had much more power and influence than he realized.

To get him thinking about how he could create the outcome that he wanted, I asked him a few questions. Even though you may be faced with a different type of opportunity or challenge than his, the following questions will shift your mindset and approach—leading you closer to the outcome you want:

- **What would you like to have happen?**

  Start by defining what the ideal outcome would look like. *Get really specific about the most important elements,* for you and the other party involved. For example, these elements could include your role and responsibilities, your working relationship with the other party, your compensation, and so on.

- **What would it take to make that happen?**

  Next, for the ideal outcome to happen, what would it really take? In other words, what are the key pieces that would have to be in place? In the example above, it was more credibility and trust between the two parties. As we talked further, he also realized that minimizing risk for both parties mattered a great deal.

- **What are the first two steps you can take to lead to the outcome you want?**

  After you've answered the first two questions, you will find that the answer to this last question comes much more easily. You begin to see the small steps you can take to start moving things in the direction you want. Remember that it can be subtle things that you say or do. The most important part is making sure the steps tie to the outcome you want and what must be in place to make it happen. In this example, this leader realized that crafting some kind of pilot project was the best way for both parties to try something on a small scale, to minimize risk and advance their working relationship.

Although we don't always have control over a situation, we *can* influence the outcome. Just remember that getting really clear about what you want shifts your mindset and helps you naturally and easily start creating the outcome you want.

HOW TO KEEP YOUR GOOD IDEA FROM BEING SHOT DOWN

Have you ever found yourself frustrated because you have a good idea but it doesn't go anywhere? No matter how big or small the idea, we've all faced this at some point. After reading John Kotter's recent book, *Buy In—Saving Your Good Idea from Getting Shot Down*, I thought it would help to share some of his strategies to "save" good ideas.

Take stock.

Start with being crystal clear about your idea. Can you explain your idea in a short elevator ride? If not, you need to distill it down to the essential elements, while keeping it simple. Don't let yourself get bogged down in giving so much context or justification for your idea that you lose your audience in the details. Think about the basics of what they need to know.

Next, think about who might support the idea, and which likely supporters you should talk to about the idea before sharing it more broadly. I remember from my years at Deloitte Consulting, this strategy was invaluable for getting buy-in and for identifying potential attacks, and who they might come from. So, think about how you can engage your supporters to respond to naysayers, and ask them about when and how you should communicate to key stakeholders. If you do it right, the decision-making meeting should be a non event—because you had all the right meetings before the meeting.

Finally, role-play the meeting or conversation in advance, anticipating and responding to attacks or objections. Sometimes it can really help to have someone brainstorm with you.

Anticipate the four basic attack strategies.

Although the book lists 28 attack strategies, at the core they are all about the following four basic attack strategies:

1. **Fear mongering** – This strategy aims at raising anxieties of the group to prevent a thoughtful examination of the idea. It gets people responding irrationally and emotionally.

2. **Death by delay** – You may have experienced this frustrating strategy firsthand. This is where so many meetings or steps are

proposed that you completely miss the window of opportunity for the idea.

3. **Confusion** – This tactic muddies the water with irrelevant facts, convoluted logic, or so many alternatives that a productive dialogue gets stalled.

4. **Ridicule and character assassination** – This is what I call playing dirty, whether it's through verbal or nonverbal communication. The attacker may raise questions about your competence or preparation, redirecting the conversation away from the idea itself.

Develop your responses in advance.

So, what should you do to respond to these attack strategies? In a nutshell, Kotter recommends doing the unexpected, taking the high road, and staying focused. Here are the four elements he suggests you integrate into your response.

1. Let attackers into the discussion and let them go after you. Kotter suggests doing this because it gets people's attention. Without their attention, you won't have a chance to explain the issue or your proposed solution.

2. Keep your responses clear, simple, crisp, and full of common sense. Don't get mired in explaining all the logic and facts, which can make any audience glaze over.

3. Show respect constantly. Don't fight or collapse or become defensive. By treating others with respect, you draw an audience emotionally to your side, where they are more likely to listen carefully and sympathetically.

4. Focus on the whole audience. Don't be distracted by the detractors. Remember that it's about winning the hearts and minds of the majority, not the minority.

At the end of the day, it's all about preparation. You can use these concepts to prepare before you pitch any idea—no matter how big or small because the basic approach is sound. Just don't try to wing it, even if your idea seems bulletproof or you expect a friendly audience. A few minutes of preparation can go a long way.

THE IMPACT OF THE COMPANY YOU KEEP

I do a lot of speaking about building a network of powerful advocates, something that women often underestimate. When you really take time to think about it, who you surround yourself with makes a huge difference. Today I want you to take a few minutes to think about *your* network and how you might strengthen it. As you think about the three questions below consider the people you currently rely on, on a regular basis (e.g., your core network).

1. **Do they look like you?**

    One of the most valuable things you can do is surround yourself with people who can challenge your ideas and bring different perspectives. How many of the people in your core network look like you with similar thinking styles, perspectives, and experiences? If most are like you, you may be inadvertently limiting your ideas.

2. **Do they extend your expertise?**

    Another important dimension that you may underestimate is expertise. To what extent do the people in your network, whether personal or professional contacts, expand your knowledge and understanding? Do they work in different industries? How much can you learn from them?

3. **Do they span different levels?**

    Finally, knowing people at different levels of the hierarchy can benefit you immensely. Consider for a moment the value a network like this would hold if you were leading a change effort across the company and needed to get the pulse of the organization. It could also bring forward new ideas and perspectives from people who are closer to the day-to-day business activity. Don't forget to consider leaders with power and influence, a group that women often focus less on. Remember that they can be valuable advocates and resources to get things done.

As you read the questions above, what jumped out at you about your own network? Where do you see opportunities to strengthen it? Remember the breadth of your network impacts your diversity of thought, knowledge, access to resources, and ability to get things done quickly.

So, your challenge is to identify one person that you would like to strengthen a relationship with in the next six months and the first step you will take to do so. Remember that small steps can lead to big results.

TINY TRAPS THAT REDUCE YOUR EFFECTIVENESS

In a conversation with one of my former colleagues from Deloitte, we got on the topic of little things that people do that diminish their effectiveness. It's amazing how seemingly small things can make a big impression. Take a look at the list below to see if any of these apply to you. If you're not sure, ask others for feedback:

1. **Assume That Others Understand**

    Sometimes when you have worked in an industry or functional area for so long, you can easily overlook how much jargon you use or the complexity of your world. So, periodically confirm that the other person understands your train of thought and the technical terms you are using. If you're on the receiving end of the confusing jargon, ask questions in the spirit of making sure you understand their key points.

2. **Focus More on Your Own Message**

    Have you ever found yourself chomping at the bit to get your point across while someone is talking? Maybe you're just really excited about your idea or you strongly disagree with what the other person is saying. If you fall into this trap often, practice being "in the moment" to fully receive the communication from the other person—not only their words but what they are saying with their body language and tone. This may ultimately lead you to an ever better idea.

3. **Immediately Show Your Feelings on Your Face**

    At one time or another, we've all found our faces showing exactly what we feel:

    - You just don't get it—and you never will!"

    - "You're an idiot. That was the dumbest thing I have ever heard anyone say!"

    - "You are so irritating."

    - "I don't have time for this. What do you want?!"

As you think about the last time a situation like this occurred, ask yourself a few questions.

- What was the impact of your reaction?
- How did it affect your effectiveness as a leader (e.g., the relationship with the person, results, etc.)?
- What assumptions did you make?

If you can make yourself pause even for a second or two, you may be able to contemplate a different possibility—that they have positive intentions, that they may have valid points, or that your assumptions may be incorrect. So, instead of judging, what could you ask them to confirm your understanding about their intent, goals, or point of view?

4. Use "Filler" Phrases

As you move further and further up the ladder, clear and concise communication matters a *lot*. Filler phrases like these—and, so, actually, um, right—can detract from your message, especially when you use them over and over.

I discovered mine when I recorded my new program. Yes, it's always enlightening to hear yourself speak! Unless you have the opportunity to hear a recording of yourself, ask others to tell you what they notice and how it impacts your effectiveness.

I challenge you to identify one tiny trap that you might fall into. If you're not sure, ask for feedback. I want to help you notice the little things that add up to a lot—and be much more intentional about how you "show up." Remember that taking small steps to improve your effectiveness can go a long way.

THREE IMPORTANT QUESTIONS
TO ASK YOURSELF

I had the opportunity to hear from several leaders at the national Women's Foodservice Forum (WFF) Conference through panel discussions, keynote speeches, and breakout sessions. The conference theme was "Aspire Higher." Their wisdom and reminders prompted me to ask you these three questions this week:

1. **Are you "living" your goals?**

   Carin Stutz, CEO of Cosi and WFF Chair, kicked of the conference by challenging us to think about whether we are truly "living" our goals. If you're like most people, you may get caught up in the day-to-day flurry of life, and not stop to evaluate whether your goals and actions are in sync. *Even taking five minutes to reflect on this can raise your awareness and help you recognize major gaps.* If some do exist, identify one step you can take to move in the right direction. For example, many of my clients carve out time each week to reflect (even if it's just starting with 15 minutes), to help them maintain their focus.

2. **How often do you accept help?**

   Karen Williams; Executive Director Strategy Implementation at Applebee's Services, Inc. advised, "When someone offers to help, be brave enough to take it." Especially for those of you high performing women who are used to being self-reliant and self-sufficient, it can take a lot of courage to do this.

   Think about what prevents you from asking for or accepting help. Maybe you don't want to impose or be viewed as incapable? Or you have perfectionist tendencies? *Keep in mind that allowing others to help is not just about you.* When you accept help, you give others the opportunity to make a difference, develop their skills, or get exposure—things that matter to them.

3. **Do you have a sustainability plan?**

   One of the speakers talked about the importance of a "sustainability plan." I have to say this was the first time I had ever heard anyone use the term for an individual versus an organization. But when I think about it, it makes a lot of sense. *At the end of the day, this is about heading down a path that will give you the opportunities you want but will also be sustainable.*

So, what will you do to maintain focus on what matters most to you personally and professionally? What is your game plan to make sure you that have the support you need, get enough sleep and exercise, and proactively manage your energy?

Identify one small step you can take in one of the three areas above. You know I'm a firm believer that small steps can lead to big results.

DO YOU RECOGNIZE THE IMPACT OF YOUR STRENGTHS?

After facilitating a couple of workshops based on the book, *Strategically Standing Out* by Marcus Buckingham, I continue to notice that high performers often take their own strengths, or the impact of their strengths, for granted. If you consider your strengths as a mere reflection of "who you are" rather than something that truly sets you apart, read on.

Unlike *Now, Discover Your Strengths*, which focuses on individual strengths, *Strategically Standing Out* talks about Strengths Roles. Buckingham has identified nine roles that reflect a combination of your talents and skills and describe how you instinctively provide value. The roles are derived from a timed assessment that asks how you would respond in a variety of situations.

As we all know, identifying your top Strengths Roles is just the beginning. *To really put them into play you have to understand what they really mean for you—their* **impact.** Whether or not you decide to take the assessment, try this simple exercise.

1. Identify your top three strengths, or top two Strengths Roles (if you take the assessment).

2. For each, describe what you say and do when you are playing to that strength or Strengths Role.

3. Identify the impact.

Let me bring this to life with an example of a client, who we'll call Susan.

Strengths Role:

Susan is a Connector, someone who brings ideas, things, or people together to make something bigger and better (refer to *Strategically Standing Out* for more details on being a Connector).

What she says and does when she's playing to this strength/Strengths Role:

Susan listens, asks thought-provoking and targeted questions, absorbs information, eliminates the "noise," and sees linkages that others don't see. She also consistently introduces people who would benefit from meeting each other.

The impact:

Susan has insights that others don't have. She helps the team focus on the core issues buried within the information they have, which helps them make faster decisions with her involvement.

She has strong relationships and a solid network of support, which helps her get things done faster given her access to valuable information, people, and resources. Susan initiates collaboration where none would otherwise have existed.

Remember, it's much harder to help others understand how to leverage your strengths (or for you to integrate your strengths into your leadership brand) if you don't understand them yourself. If you believe that success comes more from playing to your strengths, rather than focusing most of your efforts on improving your development areas, consider reading *Strategically Standing Out*.

If nothing else, try the simple exercise above this week and discuss it with someone who knows you well. You might be surprised at the impact you are having—on others and results.

DO YOU USE SELF-PROMOTION AS A LEADERSHIP TOOL?

I speak on the topic of tasteful self-promotion all the time. I have to say that this is truly a timeless topic because most women and some men struggle with how to do it. I even have an entire module dedicated to it my "*WOW! Women On the Way to Peak Performance Program*^{SM}."

As one of the faculty for the George W. Bush Presidential Center's inaugural Women's Initiative Fellowship Program, I had a chance to teach fourteen women from Egypt how to do this. Although they debated with me about whether self-promotion was something they could do in a way that fit with their culture and was aligned with their personal styles and values, the women successfully developed and implemented strategies that worked for them during their four weeks in the United States. So, I'm here to tell you that if fourteen women from Egypt can do it, so can you!

Here's a quick self-assessment you can take to help you determine where you might have some opportunities to be more effective. Rate yourself on the following eight statements using the scale below:

1 = Not at all; 2 = Very little; 3 = Neutral;
4 = To a moderate extent; 5 = To a great extent

1. I view self-promotion in a positive light.
2. I am comfortable self-promoting.
3. I know who needs to know about my accomplishments and results.
4. The "right" people know how I add value.
5. I notice and track my accomplishments.
6. I am armed with quick stories I can tell.
7. I have a 30-60 second elevator speech.
8. I spend at least five minutes/week to toot my own horn.

As you can see from the statements above, it all starts with your mindset. Most people view tooting their own horns as bragging, self-centered, or just plain obnoxious. And I would agree that the most memorable examples of self-promotion tend to be negative. However, there are many people who do use self-promotion as an effective tool to demonstrate their leadership.

Rather than taking a negative view, I urge you to reframe self-promotion as a valuable way to inform others and to help them learn from what you have accomplished. When you view it this way, it becomes less about you and more about providing something relevant and useful to others.

Next, think about how you want to "show up" in a conversation where you do tell others about your accomplishments and results. How do you want to be viewed? What is important to you? Answering these questions will help you frame your achievements in a way that works for you and choose the right words, which will make it much easier for you to tastefully self-promote.

Finally, take a look at your responses to the assessment above. What did you notice, and what action do you want to take? You could start by clarifying what stops you from self-promoting, identifying who needs to know about your accomplishments, or simply jotting down examples of your achievements and results.

I challenge you to identify one small step to get the ball rolling this week. You know I'm a firm believer that small steps can lead to big results.

THE VALUE OF BEING "SPEECHLESS"

I remember the time when I lost my voice to the point of a whisper. It was truly a first for me. As an extrovert and someone who provides coaching and consulting services, it was *so* hard to refrain from talking. To add another interesting dimension, I also had my six-year-old son solo that weekend, so writing down what I wanted to say wasn't an option—unless of course I wanted to limit myself to simple three-letter or four-letter words!

So, between losing my voice and starting off that week teaching coaching skills to a group of leaders, it reminded me of two simple but important ideas relevant to leadership.

1. **Notice themes in your nonverbal communication.**

    Sometimes we forget how much we communicate without ever uttering a word. Whether it's that scowl on your face, the hand on your hip, or that big smile—you constantly send messages. And the nonverbal cues speak so much louder than words, carrying much more weight if there's a "disconnect" between the two.

    So, right now, take a minute to think about what you are communicating on a day-to-day basis. Do you constantly look rushed, stressed out, or too busy to stop and have a conversation? How do your nonverbal messages align with your leadership brand (i.e., what you want to be known for as a leader)? If you are unsure about what you're communicating nonverbally, ask for feedback from people you trust.

2. **Recognize how the simple act of listening can propel things forward.**

    During the session I facilitated yesterday, I helped leaders practice coaching skills that they can apply to any role or situation. As you might expect, we focused on listening as one of those critical skills. Through various coaching scenarios and interactive role play, the leaders focused on:

    - Giving their undivided attention
    - Being "in the moment"
    - Listening with genuine curiosity

- Withholding judgment as they listened

As we talked about the experience, several leaders mentioned how listening in this way can make a huge difference *because the other person feels heard.* They went on to say how taking this approach generated more engagement, opened the other person up to exploring solutions, and ultimately helped them take action faster.

Think about this for a minute. As a leader, if your team members feel that you are willing to listen *and* care about their perspectives, they will get more engaged in solving their own problems—giving you more capacity to work on other priorities.

So, right now, look at the questions below to assess how effectively you listen:

- How often do you multi-task as others are talking?
- How much do you focus on how you would solve the person's problem or what you would say next while the other person is talking?
- How much do you *really* pay attention to the person's tone of voice, energy, nonverbal cues, and words?

Hopefully these two simple reminders have made you pause, as I did that week, to consider a small tweak you'd like to make. I urge you to identify one small step you'll take in the next five days to align your nonverbal communication with your leadership brand or to fine tune your listening skills. Remember, small steps can lead to big results.

HOW WELL DO YOU MANAGE YOUR ENERGY?

I specialize in working with high performing leaders, people who have high expectations of themselves and won't settle for less. When work gets really demanding, a high performer often responds by working longer hours, sometimes to the point of getting sick or disillusioned.

Research shows that proactively managing your energy can increase your capacity to get things done and improve your well-being (see HBR article: *Manage Your Energy, Not Your Time*). This is a lesson I learned the hard way a few years ago at Deloitte when I was leading a high stakes, high visibility initiative for the firm. Since then, I have helped many leaders develop strategies to renew their energy on a daily basis to avoid burnout and get better results.

To understand how well *you* manage your energy, look at each statement below and note whether it is True or False for you.

1. I rarely get eight hours of sleep each night.
2. I exercise less than three times per week.
3. I often skip meals or eat unhealthy food.
4. I constantly deal with interruptions at work, leaving little time to focus on what I need to do.
5. I have little time to reflect so I can be more proactive at work.
6. I have difficulty shutting work off after business hours and on
7. I feel stressed out and irritable, especially when I'm under pressure.
8. There is a gap between what I think is important and how I actually spend my time.
9. When I do spend time with my family, I'm not fully there.
10. I don't spend enough time doing what I really enjoy or find fulfilling.

The point of this exercise is not to depress you, but rather to give you a quick snapshot of how you are doing. From the list above, choose one area that you would like to improve and identify one action that you will take this week to get started. Take a look at the examples below:

*   I am going to leave my desk for lunch today
*   I will exercise today, even if it is just for 15 minutes

- I will go to bed 20 minutes earlier than I usually do
- I will listen to some good music on the drive home instead of taking another conference call, so I can unplug from work by the time I get home
- I will not check email after 6:30 PM today

Hopefully these examples will provoke some simple ideas for you. Just get started and you'll notice that your energy level and results improve. Remember, small steps can lead to big results.

HOW TO STOP WORKING ALL THE TIME

At the University of Houston's Women's Studies Table Talk 2010 event, I facilitated an invigorating discussion about how we live in a 24/7, "give me what I'm asking for right now" world. Many of us work in companies with a high performance, immediate response culture which makes it _so_ hard to stop working all the time. Well I'm here to tell you that it is possible to stop work from taking over your life if you *start with what you can control.* Here are four simple strategies to get you started.

1. **Recognize your mindset.**

    Your mindset plays a huge role in all of this. I'll give you an example. A retired nurse at our table asked a great question, "Why can't something wait until tomorrow? In nursing, if you don't get everything done during your shift, a patient could die. I just don't understand what can't wait in business."

    As you know, when you're "in it," it is so hard to see how crazy it might look or sound from an outside perspective. It's hard to keep in mind that for most of us, in our jobs no one will die if everything doesn't get done today. Just remember to focus on completing what does matter the most. In the end, that's what really counts.

2. **Help others see your focus on business goals and results.**

    Do you worry about what others will think if you start setting boundaries? For example, will others look at how you work (e.g., your hours or schedule, and whether you're in the office or working at home) as a bigger indicator of your commitment and performance than your actual results? For example, if you leave work at 5:00 every day, even if you don't have a socially acceptable excuse like a child to pick up, will they think you're just not working hard enough even if you're getting the job done?

    If this sounds familiar, think about how you can proactively communicate and manage up. Just remember that others, including your boss, are far too busy to notice everything you're doing, so what they do see is often their picture of reality. Be strategic about providing positive snapshots of your performance—but do it with integrity and authenticity. For example, keep them regularly informed about important issues and how you are managing through them, or your progress on a key business goal.

3. Set personal boundaries.

Setting personal boundaries that allow you to maintain your energy and productivity is critical. Let's look at a couple of examples. A woman at our table agreed to start turning off her BlackBerry at 8 PM every day, which will also help her stop dreaming about work! Another woman said she consistently leaves the office at 5:00 to make a 5:30 class at the gym, and she has a workout buddy meet her there (which makes it much harder not to show up). As a result, others around her know how important exercise is to her, and she has in effect "trained them" to expect her to leave at 5:00 no matter what. Both of these women will be so much more productive by setting limits that allow them to recharge, instead of just working more hours that lead to burnout.

4. Ask for help.

I know that asking for help is particularly hard if you're a high-achieving perfectionist. I will just ask you one question: When you say "yes" to doing everything perfectly, what are you saying "no" to by default? It may be exercise, time with your kids, or time for yourself—the possibilities are endless.

Perfectionist or not, I would urge you to stretch yourself to think about creative ways to ask for and get help. Remember, there are plenty of eager young professionals out there wanting to develop themselves, even if they don't report directly to you.

I'd like to end this article with a Call to Action. Pick one of the four areas above to start with, and find someone to hold you accountable for whatever action step you decide to take. You might be surprised that once you start making changes to stop working all the time, others may be eager to make changes too.

YOU DON'T NEED A CLONE—JUST MAKE THE MOST OF YOUR TIME

Do you ever wish there were more hours in the day or that you could clone yourself to get all your work done? Unfortunately, no matter how you slice it or dice it, there are still just 24 hours in each day. So, the key question is, "How can you make the most of the time you do have?"

1. **Assess**

   First, evaluate how you are currently spending your time. A simple way to do this is by creating an activity log with four columns: time of day, activity, time spent, and priority. In the last column, rate the priority of each activity as a 1, 2, or 3:

   1 = Critical (high value, directly related to achieving a critical goal)
   2 = Moderate (medium value, indirectly related to achieving a critical goal and has urgency)
   3 = Low (low value, may include urgent and non urgent tasks)

   Try to keep this log for a week with as much detail as possible. If that sounds like too much, shoot for at least three days, choosing days that are representative of a typical day for you.

   Next, review your log to determine how much time you are spending on critical activities, how fragmented your time is throughout the day, where you are wasting time, and whether you are taking enough breaks to maintain your productivity. Once you have a sense of how you are spending your time, you can more effectively develop strategies to make better use of it.

2. **Prioritize and Protect**

   Before each day begins (ideally at least one day ahead of time), identify up to three critical tasks that you need to get accomplished that day. Critical tasks are defined as tasks that move you towards achieving critical goals. Really challenge yourself to think about what's critical versus urgent.

   Next, think about whether you will need a dedicated block of time to complete these tasks based on how much creativity, thought and challenge is required. Then block the time on your calendar and protect it! Interruptions can be huge time wasters. A temporary shift in attention from one task to another can increase the amount of time necessary to finish the primary task by as much as 25 percent! So, staying focused on one thing can make a huge difference.

I think it's safe to assume that you will face unplanned interruptions and distractions throughout the day, but you *do* have control over how you manage them. So, think about some strategies to deal with the most frequent ones. For example, when I really need to get something done, I close my instant messaging software and email and don't answer my phone. Although that works well for me, it's important to determine what strategies will work best for you.

3.　Bundle

Finally, bundle tasks that entail a repetitive process (i.e., ones with the same sequence of steps) such as answering emails, opening mail, or creating invoices. This will allow you to complete them more efficiently as you get into the rhythm of getting them done.

By taking the time to implement these three simple strategies, you will get better results—without cloning yourself or finding a way to make time stand still.

BEING IN THE MOMENT

At my 25-year high school reunion, I found myself going back down memory lane. I had so much fun reconnecting with old friends and making new ones.

As a member of the planning committee, I found myself paying much more attention to the body language and cues at each reunion event, because I wanted to make sure that people were having a good time. As I looked around, I was surprised by how much I noticed after just a few seconds. This reminded me of the importance of truly *being in the moment.* Although in this case I'm talking about a personal situation, the same concept applies to business.

So, I want to point out three things about "being in the moment" that may be helpful to you as a leader.

1. **Notice the valuable information in front of you.**

    Day to day, most of us are so focused on our own responsibilities, that we overlook the valuable information that others send our way. Whether it's someone's look of frustration or anger or their excitement, it gives you insight into how they are feeling. More importantly, it gives you clues about how to respond in that situation.

    Let me give you an example of how someone I know has put this into play. I have a former colleague from Deloitte Consulting who has mastered the art of "noticing." When she enters a room, she quickly looks around and pays attention to the energy level and the body language of each person. So, when she speaks to someone, she already has valuable information that allows her to engage with the person beyond a surface level. She often surprises people when she mentions what she noticed, because she's usually right on.

2. **Send the right message about your leadership.**

    I remember coaching a manager who literally would have one foot out the door each time he would talk to one of his direct reports. Or even worse, he'd be looking at his BlackBerry the whole time. Yet he was surprised when his 360-feedback report said that his team feels like he doesn't have time for them and that he just cares about himself.

Although he had a busy schedule like most managers, he recognized that he couldn't get his job done without his team. On top of that, he *really did care* about them. So he decided that each morning, he would take five minutes to talk to at least one of his employees as he got his morning coffee. It was a simple strategy that helped him connect with his team before his day got crazy. By making a small investment of his time and giving each person his undivided attention, he communicated that he valued his relationships with them.

3. **Take advantage of the opportunity in front of you.**

    Finally, if your mind is distracted by something other than what's going on right now, *you may miss the opportunity in that moment*—to be creative, spontaneous, or something else. You may be so deep in thought or busy checking your PDA that you miss the chance to bring your "A" game.

Here is my Call to Action. Look at your calendar and choose an upcoming meeting to practice "being fully in the moment." When you get to the meeting, remember to put your technology away so it doesn't distract you. During the meeting, simply notice what's going on around you—the body language, tone of voice, energy, and what's being said. You may be surprised at how much you learn about others, and how much more engaged you are.

LIFE LESSONS FROM THE GRAND CANYON

In the summer of 2012, I took a spectacular five-day hiking and camping trip to the Grand Canyon. Although my trip started off a little rough as I twisted my ankle on the first day trekking down into the Canyon, our amazing guide, Chris, wrapped it so well that I didn't miss a beat.

Chris has experiences and wisdom far beyond his 28 years including practicing his survival skills on a remote island for 13 months with nothing but the clothes on his back and the shoes on his feet, and living with various Native American Indian tribes for a year and a half to learn about their heritage and practices.

On this trip, our hiking group took a huge leap of faith in his ability to keep us safe while stretching us beyond our limits. Chris said this phrase several times and it stuck with me, "Speed is safety. Hesitation kills. Confidence is key." Its relevance to the business world and life in general, is what leads me to share it with you today.

1. **Speed is safety.**
    Speed matters, whether you're striving to be first to market or meet a business goal, or trying to get to the other side of a steep cliff. To face that huge challenge you must keep moving forward. Taking a step, no matter how small, can help you learn that critical lesson or give you the ability to see things from a different vantage point.

    Although speed matters, so does rest. So, when you feel your energy draining or the signs of burnout creeping up on you, take a break—but not for too long. In other words, rest long enough to boost your energy but short enough to keep you from getting stiff and stopping entirely. You have to strike a good balance between getting rest and maintaining momentum.

2. **Hesitation kills.**
    Hesitation can be deadly. I see it kill ideas on a daily basis as that golden opportunity passes by—that moment that will never return. To bring this to life, I want to share a personal experience from my trip.

    On day three, I vividly remember holding onto a boulder as we hiked across the rocks and down into the water. I was gasping for my next breath from the sheer force of the cold air from the gushing waterfall ten feet away and blinded by water spraying into my eyes ... and tentative because of my injured ankle.

As I rubbed my eyes, sure that my contact lenses had washed away, I shouted to the person behind me, "I don't know if I can do this!" As I stood there getting pounded by the water and wind, I knew I couldn't hesitate any longer because my indecision was only fueling my fear. Little did I know that it would take only six more steps to get to the other side of what we came to affectionately call "The Jacuzzi." And just six steps away was one of the most beautiful views of Avatar Falls (appropriately named by Chris, in honor of the movie), a view that I would have missed if I had hesitated any longer.

So the next time you find yourself thinking twice or being held back by fear, envision what could be on the other side. What would it really feel like if you achieved that important goal? What would it feel like if you took that leap of faith? All I can say is that I am so glad I took those additional six steps, not only for the view but also because it meant I had conquered my fear.

3. **Confidence is key.**

Confidence plays a huge role in how you view yourself, how others view you, and whether you succeed or fail. Often, stepping out with confidence is more about gathering the information you need to mitigate risk and less about self-doubt.

For example, if you're standing on land wondering whether you should jump through the waterfall into the water below, you might ask, "Where are the rocks? How deep is the water? How strong is the current, and what should I do if I get caught in it?"

Similarly, if you're wondering whether the time is right to share your "big idea" or ask for resources, make a list of the questions for which you need answers, anticipate the resistance you might encounter, and develop a game plan.

As I reflected about this trip, I realized what an amazing opportunity it truly was. Just remember that you don't have to go all the way to the Grand Canyon to seize opportunities. *They are right in front of you every day.* So, I want to challenge you to seize the next one—no matter how small—with speed and confidence, and without hesitation.

LOOK FOR THE OPPORTUNITIES RIGHT IN FRONT OF YOU

I can't tell you how often I hear people complain that they don't have time to focus on something important to them. There can be several reasons they don't dedicate the time or make the effort. For some, fear holds them back. For others, the sense of urgency isn't there. But in many cases, people simply do not see the opportunities in front of them to make progress on what they want.

So, I work with my clients to develop ways to achieve their goals without adding layers of work—which is key to getting the ball rolling. Below are three simple steps you can take. Think about each of these in the context of what you really want to accomplish.

1. **Review what is already on your calendar.**

   To get started, look 1-2 weeks out on your schedule to see who you have meetings or calls with. You may find that you will be in front of important people with whom you want to cultivate stronger relationships or get visibility. By looking at your schedule ahead of time and in the context of your goals, you can begin to set the stage for making progress on what you'd like to accomplish.

2. **Think about how you can make the most of that time.**

   Next, think about how you can make the most of the opportunity whether it's a meeting, phone call, or something else. For example, I have a client who has a strong internal network but wants to expand her external network. With her work and travel schedule, she doesn't have much time to participate in networking events. She'd been struggling to make time for quite a while.

   When we looked at her calendar, she noticed that she had a two-day meeting coming up. It was part of a prominent leadership program for which she had been selected and it included leaders from other organizations. So, we worked together to establish 1-2 goals for this meeting. She identified two individuals she wanted to cultivate relationships with and developed concrete actions steps to do just that. Ultimately, she got more out of the program *and* made progress on her networking goal without adding any time to her schedule.

3. Set up a structure to help you.

Finally, make this process a habit for yourself. If the thought of looking out a week or two in advance sounds overwhelming, you can still make the most of any single opportunity sitting in front of you.

Before each meeting or call you attend, take a couple of minutes to ask yourself:

- How do I want to show up (i.e., what impression do I want to leave? How can I reinforce my brand?)?
- In this forum, how can I also make progress against one of my goals or priorities?
- What one action will I take in this meeting or call?

My clients can attest that this really works! So, set aside time to strategically look at your calendar and set goals for your upcoming meetings and calls. As a first step, pick just one meeting in the next week to try this approach. If you're really adventurous, block 15-20 minutes on your calendar each week to strategize about the following week's meetings. You will show up with much more intention and may be surprised at the results you get.

NETWORKING FOR RESULTS

When we expanded our business into the Dallas/Ft. Worth area, several people commented on how quickly we plugged into the business community here and asked what we did to make it happen. So, I thought I'd share three simple, effective strategies that have worked for us and our clients.

1. **Get clear.**

   Networking can be a full time job if you let it. So before you dive in, clarify what you want to accomplish personally and professionally. *Developing specific goals will help you focus on who and what matters most, make the best use of your time, and make networking feel less overwhelming.*

   Let me give you a recent example. Last week, I spoke to a leader (let's call her Susan) who told me that she really needs to start networking but finds it draining and difficult. Given her busy schedule, she just doesn't know how to make it happen. So, I asked her what she was trying to accomplish. Susan explained that she wants to stay at her company, is ready to take on a bigger role, but cannot travel extensively. She admitted that her ideal role may be difficult to get at her company, so she will need strong sponsors to make it happen.

   In particular, there are two leaders who could strongly influence her career path. So, Susan needs to make sure that they know who she is and how she is adding value. As a backup plan, Susan needs to build her external network to identify opportunities outside her company. Because we clarified Susan's goals first, she could quickly develop a list of people she needs to network with internally and externally.

2. **Be consistent.**

   Most people focus on their networks when they need something. They typically view networking as optional versus core to achieving their goals. If this sounds all too familiar, I would urge you to set aside time each week to strengthen your network. Remember that it doesn't have to be time consuming. Even 5-10 minutes per week can go a long way. For example, in less than five minutes, you can send a quick email about an event or article of interest, make an introduction to someone they would enjoy meeting, or ask for advice or input.

As you develop your strategies, think about what would be of service to the person you are cultivating a relationship with. Whatever your approach, communicate regularly so that you stay top of mind.

3. Show your stuff.

Actions speak much louder than words, so I would argue that the best way for people to get to know you is by seeing you in action. *Volunteer for something that showcases your strengths, fits with your passion, and helps you develop strong relationships with the right people.* By getting involved, others will notice how you think and the value that you bring—as long as you follow through on your commitments. Otherwise, you risk damaging versus advancing the relationship. Again, you don't have to invest a lot of your time, but be clear about how much time you can give and carve out something manageable.

Because networking can feel overwhelming, start by developing one achievable goal. For example, you could carve out ten minutes this week to clarify what you want to achieve through networking. If you already know, invest those ten minutes instead to reach out to someone you want to strengthen a relationship with. Remember to look for opportunities within what is already on your calendar (e.g., meetings, calls, etc.), rather than adding more to do's to your list!

ARE YOU KEEPING YOUR GOLD MINE OF IDEAS TO YOURSELF?

If you have a useful idea and no one knows about it, does it really have any value? Well, I would argue that it doesn't. If you find yourself holding back, what makes you reluctant to speak up? It usually starts with that fleeting thought that goes through your head.

Let's take a look at three thoughts that might prevent you from sharing your views, and what you can do about each of them so that others *can* benefit from the value you bring.

"What I have to say is nothing earth shattering."

If you fall into this category, take a second to ask yourself what others could gain from your perspective. Recognize that others don't bring the same experiences you do, and what you see may not be as obvious to others (especially if they're immersed in the issue/topic).

You may be dismissive when you have truly mastered a skill (i.e., you are unconsciously competent in performing it) or have deep expertise, *because you know it like the back of your hand.* Don't underestimate the value you bring. While you may feel like you're speaking for the sake of it, remember that others may find your comments insightful and relevant.

Whether or not you say anything new or insightful by your own standards, I want to remind you that there is tremendous value in being able to:

- Summarize: This can help others in the room get refocused on what has been accomplished in the discussion and what still needs attention.
- Bring people back to the big picture: Helping them connect the dots can refocus on what's most important to the discussion at hand (especially if it's been meandering).
- Help a group see common ground: Noticing the alignment and common goals can help the whole group move forward, particularly when a range of perspectives have been shared.

"My idea is not ready for prime time."

You may hear this from people who prefer to reflect before they share their ideas with others (often introverts). Unlike extroverts who typically think and process out loud, introverts often want to be more thoughtful about what they say *before they say it*. At times this can be misconstrued as holding back ideas that could be of value to others, or perfectionism. If any of this sounds familiar, trust me you're not alone.

I would recommend that before you walk into a meeting; anticipate what might come up. What might they ask? What challenges may come up based on who will be present in the room? How would you respond? Taking even five minutes to prepare ahead of time will help you step out there a little sooner than you typically would, and with a stronger sense of conviction and confidence.

"Is this really worth my time and energy to share my views?"

Yes, we all have those moments where we are just ready for a meeting to be over. Of course you wouldn't dare bring something else up because it may drag your unproductive meeting out even longer (and it's already been going on long enough)!

Before you mentally disengage and start answering email on your BlackBerry, ask yourself what opportunity sits before you in this meeting? Remember that it's up to *you* to see these moments as unique opportunities to accomplish something of importance to you and/or your team—whether it's reinforcing your leadership brand, bringing direction to the group, advancing a relationship, or actually making productive use of an otherwise useless meeting.

I would ask you to identify *one* thing you need to keep in mind or do so that others can get value from what *you* uniquely bring. Don't keep that gold mine of ideas all to yourself. Spread the wealth.

THE POWER OF LETTING GO

During a presentation I gave in Dallas on resilience, I led the group through an exercise where they had to pull out the most valuable lessons they had learned from difficult situations they had successfully worked through in the past. I want to share a common theme that emerged from our discussion that evening—the Power of Letting Go—because I see this come up all the time with high performers.

A woman who attended my presentation described a time when she had been working and pushing so hard to resolve a critical business issue. She explained how much was at stake in this particular situation, and that she really needed some key players to step up and take action. But they just weren't getting engaged or responding as she had hoped. She worried about things unraveling, as any of us would in her situation. But she had also reached the point where there really was nothing more she could do. She went on to explain that at this low point for her, another leader in the organization gave her the following words of wisdom, "Just let go and let things happen."

Have you ever found yourself in a similar situation? As a high performer, you may do *whatever it takes* to make something work, even when it means working crazy hours and jumping through hoops. For an outsider looking in, it may appear completely insane. "Failure" probably isn't even in your vocabulary, and you may keep pushing and working harder because that has always worked for you . . . until you encounter a situation where that approach just won't work.

As a high performer, you may not recognize that your drive for results may keep others from experiencing the consequences of their choices and actions. Think about it for a minute. Why would someone jump in and do something when you're so willing to take charge and do it for them?

Just remember that what you *don't do* can be just as or more important than what you do. As I've admitted before, I too have learned from the School of Hard Knocks—and it helps me relate to what my clients face. I remember realizing the Power of Letting Go at two key points in my 14-year career at Deloitte. I recall feeling exhausted, frustrated, and burned out both times. Then I realized that doing more of the same just wouldn't get me to a different result. There was nothing left to do other than stop trying so hard—and just let go. In 2010, I experienced this lesson again as I worked through some personal transitions. I am always amazed at how letting go leads me so much faster to what I want, personally or professionally.

So, I want to leave you with three things that have helped me and my clients realize the Power of Letting Go:

1. **Recognize when you have done everything you reasonably could have to work through the challenge at hand.**

   Usually when you are working this hard, others can see your commitment, work ethic, and drive for results. The question is, "Do you see it?" Look for the evidence.

2. **Ask yourself what could happen if you stopped pushing so hard.**

   Take time to think about the consequences others might experience and the ripple effect of those, if you stopped pushing so hard. And don't forget to think about how letting go would impact you.

3. **Take a leap of faith that things will work out as they should.**

   There may be some things you don't know or just can't see about the situation because you are so immersed in it. Just let them unfold. Trust that if you have acted in good faith and given it your best shot, the outcome will be what it should be.

So, the next time you find yourself in a tough situation and pushing really hard, keep these three things in mind. You might be surprised at how letting go will help you take a giant leap forward.

WHAT IS "SITTING ON THE FENCE" COSTING YOU?

Have you ever found yourself sitting on the fence about something that's really important to you? It could be related to a career decision, going for what you want personally or professionally, or making an investment in yourself. *Well, I'm here to tell you that the road ahead is full of new opportunities and possibilities . . . and you can make some different choices than you have in the past.*

I have the privilege of working with talented leaders every day to help them get results they couldn't before. And what I often see is that despite their success, at times even they find themselves sitting on the fence instead of moving forward. Here are three common traps they fall into:

1. **This isn't a good time.**

   This is what I like to call "playing it safe." There are so many reasons to stay *exactly where we are and not take action.* The lists are endless. Do any of these sound familiar?

   - "If I can just finish this project or get past the next two months, then I'll have time to focus on this."

   - "There's already been a lot of change in the company. I don't want to rock the boat."

   - "I can't ask for the company to invest in a coach or a training program for me, even if I can quickly recoup the investment. Budgets are tight.

   Whether the reason is time, money, or something else; it's up to you to make the business case:

   - What *does* make this the right time to take action?
   - What positive outcomes could occur if I move forward now instead of waiting?
   - What's at risk personally or professionally, if I wait?

2. **I need more information**

   If you find yourself in an endless cycle of gathering and analyzing data, the question to ask yourself is "What do I *have to know* to move forward with this?" By focusing on the one or two most critical things, you can put aside the "nice to have" but less important information that's muddying the water. We will never have all the information we want or need, so use the 80/20 rule and focus on the 20 percent that matters the most.

3. **What if it doesn't work out? Or, what if it does?**

Sometimes the fear of getting what you want can be scarier than the fear of not getting it—because at the end of the day, it means change. And change is hard, even when it's positive. So, you may find yourself lacking energy and enthusiasm to move forward, even when it's something that really matters to you.

Ask yourself, "If I move forward with this, what could happen? What would be different?" Play out your worst case and your best case scenarios as if you were watching them on video. Describe what is happening in as much detail as possible. By playing them out, you will get a better sense of how likely they are to happen and what's really underlying your fear.

Just remember that we all find ourselves sitting on the fence at one point or another. The key is to not be there long enough to get splinters. Whether your response is a "yes" or a "no" on whether to move forward on something that really matters to you, sometimes it's important to just make a decision. So answer the questions above, and consider working with a coach or someone who can help you figure out what's making you hesitate. That's the first step to getting off that fence.

CAN YOU REALLY AFFORD NOT TO ASK FOR HELP?

One of the common themes I find in coaching high performing women managers and leaders is their reluctance to ask for help. This shows up in their personal and professional lives. As you know, women are socialized to take care of others, so naturally it can be easier to put everyone else's needs ahead of their own.

In the working world, this can limit a woman's ability to take her performance and career to the next level. When combined with the added demands of a family, especially a two-career family, it also dramatically increases the risk of burnout. This has huge implications for women, and their employers.

Below are four common traps that women often fall into, and suggestions on how to reframe them so that they don't get in your way.

1. **"I should be able to do this."**

   This trap is all about having high expectations and standards for yourself, which has pros and cons. On one hand, it can drive you to consistently deliver high quality work. On the other hand, it may cause you to overlook how you can empower others, develop them to contribute more, and help them feel important. Next time you fall into this trap, ask yourself what you are indirectly communicating to others when you choose to take it all on yourself.

2. **"I like things done a certain way, so I'd rather just do it myself."**

   Is the pursuit of perfection getting in your way, whether it's about how your spouse loads the dishwasher or how a PowerPoint presentation is formatted? We all have our preferred ways of doing things, but at what cost? In the big picture, how important is it for *this* task to be done perfectly, and to be done by *you*? What higher priority items should you spend your time on instead?

3. **"It will take more time to explain this task than it would to do it."**

   This trap is all about the short-term vs. long-term trade-offs. In other words, it may take more time to delegate and explain this task *this* time, but the next time you need help it will go much faster. By investing time now, you can set the stage for getting ongoing help with this and other tasks.

4. **"Everyone's already so busy. I don't want to overload them."**

   This is the classic trap of deciding for others before you even give them a chance to weigh in on the decision. Who knows, you may find that others are too busy help. But then again, you might not. Someone may want to help you because they think what you're working on is interesting or challenging, or they just want as a chance to demonstrate their capabilities. To them, it may be worth taking on more work to have that opportunity. Trust that they will let you know if they can't help.

In the long run, taking it all on yourself can limit your success and the success of your team. *Just remember that there is an implicit trade-off in the choices you make.* Keep these traps in mind so that you make those choices consciously.

PUT YOUR NETWORK TO WORK

When people think of networking, they often think about how to expand the size of their network. This article is going to give you tips on how to harness the power of your existing network to achieve your goals.

To bring this to life, let's take an example of Susan, a client I worked with recently. When I first began coaching her, Susan was frustrated with her current job and was ready to make a career change. However, she had been so focused on doing her day- to-day work that she had invested little to no time maintaining or building her network within or outside the company. Sound familiar? Read on to learn more about the process we used to help her make a change and put her network to work:

1. **Brainstorm a list of five contacts that can help in the context of your specific goal.**

   After outlining Susan's ideal next role in marketing, we brainstormed names of five individuals she should reach out to. I challenged her to think about personal and professional relationships. Just taking ten minutes to go through this exercise helped Susan think of people she had completely overlooked.

2. **Determine the current and desired strength of your relationship with them.**

   Using a scale of 0-10, we rated the strength of Susan's existing relationship with each of these five individuals. For the people that Susan had very strong relationships with already, she rated them a "10" and for those she had never met, she rated them a "0." We also used the same scale to determine what she wanted the strength of the relationship to become over the next six months to a year. These ratings helped her focus and prioritize her efforts.

3. **Identify someone who can introduce you to the people you have not met.**

   For the individual that Susan did not personally know on her list, she identified someone in her current network that knew him or could at least help identify the right next step to meet him.

4. **Develop specific relationship-building strategies by person.**

Next, Susan and I brainstormed at least one or two strategies to further build the relationships with each of the five individuals. Sometimes, this is where people get stuck—especially if they already feel pressed for time. Just remember, networking doesn't have to be time consuming. It can be as simple as sending someone an article that's relevant to her, sharing information on an upcoming event she may want to attend, making a point to introduce yourself at a meeting, or asking her for a 15-minute meeting to get her input on something you're working on or getting career advice.

Just remember that the goal is to network in a way that is authentic for you and leaves a positive impression. So, as you develop these strategies think about what you want the other person to remember about you.

5. **Set deadlines for each strategy.**

Finally, to really put some accountability in place, I asked Susan to set deadlines for each of the networking strategies she identified. This helped her maintain focus and track progress.

I am very excited to tell you that Susan put her network to work, and got her dream job (which was also a promotion for her) in three months! She moved into a very different type of role than she has had held in the past. Even though this example is about career transition, the steps above can be applied to any goal. How do you want to put your network to work?

IS FEAR HOLDING YOU BACK?

No matter what anyone says, change takes energy—whether it's positive or negative change. We may tell ourselves that we embrace change and thrive on it, but the reality is that it can be stressful. Change often triggers fear, one of the biggest impediments to success.

So, what is fear exactly? At the most basic level, fear is resistance. Let's take the simple analogy of a thermostat to further explore this. We are living creatures with systems that operate in a narrow range. For example, the human body temperature is 98.6 degrees and blood pressure falls within a specific range. So, in essence, your body has a particular "setting" on a thermostat. If you change that setting even half a point, your body has to expend energy—so your body "resists" in order to conserve your energy and keep you exactly where you are. When you are trying to make a change in your behavior, a similar process occurs. Fear and other discouraging thoughts show up in order to keep things status quo.

So, how can you keep fear from holding you back? Here are five strategies to consider:

1. **Tame your Gremlins.**

   The "Gremlin" is the internal voice that makes us have second thoughts or fear change. For example, your Gremlin might say "You'll never find another job that pays this well and has this level of flexibility." *Realize that the Gremlin does not always speak the truth. Its function is to keep things exactly as they are—to stop you from making the change.* Pay close attention to what your Gremlin says to you, and develop strategies to counter its voice. Depending on your circumstances, the Gremlin may be very powerful and you might need outside help to reduce the power of its voice.

2. **Take small steps.**

   Break change down into manageable pieces and tackle each piece one at a time. This will break down your resistance, and make the change feel less insurmountable.

3. **Identify what is holding you back. Be specific.**

   Let's take the example of a man whose stomach turns upside down at the thought of giving a presentation. What triggers his fear? When he starts to think about it, he realizes that his fear surfaces only in presentations to his boss or peers. After we dig a little deeper, he realizes that at the heart of it, his fear is really about appearing incompetent in front of his colleagues. Now he has something concrete he can work to overcome.

4. **Play out your fear and develop a rational response.**

   Play out a video of your worst fear. What is happening? How likely is it that what you see in the video will happen? What is the size of the risk (large, medium, small), and the probability of it occurring (high, medium, low)? If your fear came true, how would you handle it?

   When we go through these questions, we often recognize that what we have imagined is far worse than what might happen! But even if our worst fear came true, having a game plan can make it less scary.

5. **Get support from others.**

   Don't try to take it all on by yourself. Getting help from others will make you feel like someone cares about your success. Create a support system for yourself with individuals who will encourage you and celebrate your successes—big and small.

Change can be hard work, so make sure you stack the odds in your favor. If you need some support to achieve your goals, consider working with a coach.

SECTION III

Step Out

(How Are You Using Your Leadership to Get Results and Develop Others?)

BEING STRATEGIC ABOUT
PERFORMANCE FEEDBACK

One thing I know from my experience leading Performance Management & Career Planning at Deloitte is that most people dislike giving feedback. And it can be equally challenging on the receiving end if you disagree with someone's point of view or don't understand what their feedback really means. Despite the challenges, feedback can give you valuable insight about your leadership style and strong indicators about what others value.

If you aren't taking advantage of opportunities to get input from others, here are three questions that may help you be more strategic in your approach:

1. **What should I do more or less of?**

   If you're like most people, you only focus on feedback when it's that formal time in the performance management process. Beyond that, you may have little to no conversation about how others view your business results, strengths and areas for development. If this description fits you, set aside even just 15 minutes each month to share your results and simply ask what you should be doing more or less of to be more effective. It can go a long way and you might be surprised at what you find out.

2. **How can I make it easier for others to give me feedback?**

   Be mindful of how you respond when others do give you their views, because it will impact whether they give you candid, constructive feedback in the future. Consider the following questions to help you do this:

   - How much do I focus on understanding the underlying issues or intent behind the feedback?
   - Approach the feedback from a sense of curiosity rather than judgment. Are you asking the right questions?
   - How much information do I share when responding to feedback?

- Remember that although you may be merely trying to explain your actions or behavior to others, your comments could be perceived as defensiveness.

- How well do I manage my emotions?

Visible anger, frustration, or tears can make anyone reluctant to give you feedback in the future. Recognize when you need to discontinue the conversation to allow yourself time to process the feedback.

3. **How can I make the most of feedback I disagree with?**

When I conduct 360 feedback interviews for my clients, I encourage them to focus less on whether the feedback is right or wrong and more on how it impacts their leadership effectiveness.

Remember that when there are different views of your performance, a skill gap may exist or a communication issue may exist. In other words, you may need to more consistently communicate how you are making a difference and your results.

In either case, what can you learn from the feedback? What action do you want to take as a result? And how will you follow up with people who have given their input so they know you've taken it seriously and can support you going forward?

Don't forget that feedback is all about perception, and understanding that perception can give you valuable insight to make strategic changes. Before you dive into the rest of your week, identify one step you will take to get or share information about your performance. You never know where it might lead.

PUT YOUR WISDOM TO WORK

I've noticed a theme that keeps emerging with my clients and others I meet. I've talked at length with several people about the importance of thinking big—and beyond our selves. In the midst of day-to-day life, it can be easy to forget how many people have helped us along the way, personally and professionally, and how much we have to offer.

So, instead of writing a full article on this subject, I want to challenge you to think about how you will put the power of your knowledge and wisdom to work to help someone else.

Take a look at the four questions below to get your wheels turning.

1. Who do you see struggling that could use your support?

2. Who do you see repeating the same mistakes because no one will give them the feedback they need to break the cycle?

3. Who could benefit from your influence, perspective, expertise or contacts?

4. What have you been excited about getting involved in that you just haven't taken action on?

So, before you dive back into your day, identify one thing you will do this week to pay it forward, leveraging your unique value and perspective. You might be surprised at how much you get from the experience.

ARE YOU BEING STRATEGIC ABOUT RELATIONSHIPS?

I get asked all the time about how to build a strong network of advocates. Advocates are people with power and influence who can give you important exposure, shield you from negative consequences and criticism and recommend you for new positions or visible assignments.

If you aren't paying attention to building these relationships, here are three steps to help you be more strategic about your approach:

1. **Who do you want to cultivate relationships with?**

    In the context of your professional goals, identify the top three people you need to develop stronger relationships with. They may be people you don't know at all, or are individuals who have had some exposure to you. Often they can be individuals who already have a positive impression of you, but you haven't asked them to take any action on your behalf in the past. Be specific on what you would want them to do on your behalf and make it easy for them to do so. Come prepared with the right information.

2. **What would success look like for your next conversation with them?**

    What would you want to have as the outcome of that conversation? How do you want to "show up?" In other words, think about any aspects of your brand that you'd want to focus on or what you would want them to know about you. Think about, not only your key strengths, but also experiences and results. For example: if you want to come across as competent, you can do that through the quality and caliber of the questions you ask in addition to the types of examples you share about the work you've done. Figure out what approach works best for you.

3. **What can you offer them?**

    Offer them something of value. For example, based on their interests or specific challenges they're facing, you might be able to share specific articles or resources with topics relevant to what they're dealing with. You may have contacts with similar interests who might be beneficial for them to know. You may be able to give them exposure by inviting them to speak or be on a panel in a professional association that you participate in. Or you may be able to invite them to an event that would be of interest to them.

One of the most important things to remember is to be consistent. Allocate time to focus on cultivating these relationships each month. It doesn't have to be time consuming. The key is to stay top of mind so that when opportunities do arise they will think of you. So, what step will you take this week to put this into play? Remember that small steps can lead to big results.

STRATEGIES TO CREATE A
HIGH PERFORMING TEAM

Whether you are forming a new team for a specific project or leading an existing team, there are some very practical things you can do as a leader to develop a high performing team. Here are four simple strategies to consider.

1. **Toot your own horns.**

   In the early stages, create a forum for team members to share their strengths and past experiences. This can be as simple as taking some time in a team meeting. Although some may be reluctant to toot their own horns, ask each person to share what they want others to know or understand about their background and skills, and how that information can be useful to the team. This will help each team member reach back into their past experiences, be more intentional about applying those experiences, and understand the variety and richness of the team's collective capabilities.

2. **Use the team experience to enable individual goals.**

   Take time with each individual to understand what they want to get from their participation on the team in the context of their professional goals. This will create more ownership and accountability—for you and them—as they identify what they want to get out of the team experience, and as you proactively use this information to give them exposure to the areas of expressed interest.

3. **Prevent silos.**

   Help people see beyond their areas of responsibility and notice relationships across the team. Try this simple exercise called "Visiting New Lands" to have your team walk in each other's shoes. This can apply to a department with different functional areas or an entire team with different areas of responsibility. Start by taping off and labeling a section of the floor for each functional area. Then pick a functional area to start with and have everyone physically stand in it together. Then ask all members of the team *except* for the people who work in that function to collectively answer the two questions below *as if they worked there* (e.g., if standing in the Finance section, everyone but the Finance team members would answer these questions as if they worked in Finance):

1. What are your top three challenges?
2. What are your top three priorities?

After everyone has answered the questions for that particular area, the team members who *do* work in that functional area can share their actual challenges and priorities. Then move to the next area and repeat the exercise until you have discussed each area. This exercise can provide invaluable insight into each functional area, highlight common themes across the entire team, create empathy within the team, and ignite the team's commitment to helping one another.

4. **Drive alignment through team goals.**

   Last but not least, don't underestimate the importance of having a common definition of success for your team as a whole—i.e., team goals and guidelines. This will allow you to drive alignment within the team and depersonalize differences of opinion by allowing the deciding factor to be whether something enables or detracts from the team's goals.

As you know, there are many strategies to develop a high performing team—and many of these may be reminders of what you already know. I want to challenge you to put one of these into play over the next month, if you haven't already.

THREE KEY QUESTIONS FROM DAVID NOVAK

At the 2012 sold-out national Women's Foodservice Forum (WFF) Conference in Dallas, I had the opportunity to hear David Novak, CEO of Yum! Brands and author of *Taking People with You*, speak. He shared several insights he has gained throughout his years at PepsiCo and Yum! Brands, some of which he learned from making big mistakes.

As he spoke about leadership, David reiterated that it all starts with focusing on being your best self. Not only does this mean raising your self-awareness, but also recognizing the impact you have on others and asking them for their perspective. David mentioned three important questions we should all ask:

1. **What do people appreciate about me as I am today?**

   Sometimes we take our own skills and strengths for granted, especially if we have been using them for years. Do you know how you are viewed by others, and what capabilities they really value? If not, take the time to find out what people appreciate about you and the impact you have on others, business results, and the company. The more specific the feedback, the more value you will get from it.

2. **How can I be more effective?**

   When I conduct 360-degree feedback interviews, I typically ask what my client should do more of or less of to be more effective. By asking the questions this way, I get people into a forward thinking mindset. Take the time to ask yourself and others these questions on a periodic basis to keep your own effectiveness front and center.

3. **If a "hot shot" came in to replace me today, what would he or she do?**

   This question can push you out of your day-to-day mindset. David has used it to challenge himself, incentivize fresh ideas, and seek out people who will help him elevate his game. Although you may not be able to get a meeting with Warren Buffet each year to get his thoughts as David does, you can evaluate the breadth and depth of your network and how you can stretch yourself and your team.

The three questions above will help you focus on how to put your strengths into play more powerfully, minimize less effective practices, and challenge yourself and your team. David writes the answers to the first two questions on an index card that he keeps on his desk as a constant reminder of what he should be doing. This week I want to challenge you to answer at least one of these questions. You might be surprised at what you learn about yourself.

WHAT'S YOUR IMPACT?

Every day we engage with people from all walks of life in our professional and personal lives. Each interaction results in an exchange of energy, information, and ideas—positive and negative. Through the following three questions, I challenge you today to think about the impact you have on others.

1. **What kind of energy are you giving off?**

   First, are you the kind of person who brings a conversation to a halt with your "healthy dose of realism" that others might call pessimism, or are you someone that people receive positive energy from? As you go through your day, notice how people respond to you by observing their body language, tone and actions. Recognize that some of their reactions may be more about them than you, but others may be directly related to what you are saying and doing. By paying attention more closely, you may notice some important patterns.

2. **How do you impact results?**

   Next, ask yourself how the company or others benefit from your involvement or participation, whether you're participating in a meeting or on a conference call. What do you typically contribute? Are you the person that "hangs back" or dives right in with your ideas? How much do you focus on moving things forward versus staying below the radar or just trying to wade through? Even if you're "showing up" to participate, *are you actually adding value*?

3. **What do others take from your behavior?**

   To bring the last point home, I want to share something from a meeting I was facilitating with an executive women's group last week. We talked about how leaders are always in an "invisible spotlight." In other words, people are constantly watching them, noticing what they are doing and drawing their own conclusions.

   So, whether you realize it or not, you are sending indirect messages with everything you do. What are yours? Is it that you're overwhelmed and need to be managed carefully or you might make life miserable for everyone? Or are you that unwavering leader that can provide direction and guidance consistently no matter what is going on? Recognize that small actions can add up to big messages when you put them all together.

Remember that you have an impact on everyone you interact with, but you *do* have a choice about what kind of impact you want have. So be intentional and purposeful about it and make sure that what you do reinforces your leadership brand and aligns with your values.

So, what one small step will you take this week to have the type of impact that's important to you and your team?

WHAT GUIDES YOUR LEADERSHIP?

Ask I spoke in depth with an officer at Marathon Oil about one of my clients, our discussion naturally shifted to his leadership philosophy and how it comes into play with his direct reports. I want to share the five principles from a leadership model pinned to the wall in his office. They're simple, powerful, and struck a chord with me.

1. **People want to do a good job and want to win.**

    This principle may sound really basic, but it may not be something you think about day-to-day, especially in fast-paced, stressful situations. So, the next time you find frustration creeping up on you, stop and take a deep breath. Whether you believe it or not, consider for a moment that the person you are frustrated with actually wants to do a good job. If you adopted that perspective, how might it change how you think about their behavior and how you approach the situation?

2. **People want *and deserve* to know where they stand with their supervisor.**

    I have to say that I can appreciate the difficulty most people have giving honest, constructive feedback—especially after leading Performance Management & Career Planning at Deloitte. A lot of managers and leaders dread the process and have concerns about whether the employee can handle the feedback: Will the employee have an emotional outburst? What might go wrong?

    But, as a leader, what if you viewed feedback as something people want and deserve to have? It might shift your mindset from worrying about your discomfort to providing something of value and service to your employee.

3. **Winners produce better bottom line results.**

    Research demonstrates time and again that "winners" (high performers who are *engaged*) contribute tremendously to the organizations in which they work. They creatively look for better ways to do get the job done and often elevate the performance of their entire team. *So, as a leader, ask yourself, "What 1-2 things do I need to do to create more winners?"*

4. **Managers have more impact on performance than they realize.**

Most people don't leave jobs or companies; they leave their managers. I can't tell you how often I see high performers leave organizations to work for a leader or manager they truly believe in—someone who has demonstrated that they care by supporting the employee's career goals and personally investing in their success.

Leaders with true followers typically instill in their employees a genuine desire to go above and beyond. At the end of the day, this translates into a level of commitment, loyalty, and performance that is hard to replicate.

5. **A manager's job is to produce winners.**

Ultimately, management and leadership are all about setting your employees up for success. *Great managers and leaders build a strong commitment to their organizations by investing in getting to know their employees, demonstrating that they care about their aspirations, and helping them build their capabilities.* Remember that this doesn't have to be time consuming, but it does require consistent focus.

I hope this list has stimulated some ideas for you. Before you immerse yourself into the next thing on your to do list, take a few minutes to think about what principles guide your leadership and one action you will take to reinforce just one of those principles this week. Who knows, you may end up with a list that you decide to pin up on your office wall too!

KEEP YOUR PASSION FRONT AND CENTER

When I served as a panelist for *OCA's Professional Leadership Summit: What's Passion Got to Do with It?*, I didn't realize how much I would get out of the experience. It forced me to reflect about my own career and how I've stayed in tune with what I'm passionate about over the years. I also benefited tremendously from hearing the other panelists' stories. So, I have three tips I'd like to share to help you keep your passion front and center:

1. **Set aside time to reenergize and reflect.**

    As I have analyzed my career path, I realized that every three to four years I have taken some kind of big break—a leave of absence or sabbatical—to help me get perspective and clarity about what's next for me. During that time, rather than obsessing about my career, I always focused on doing what I really enjoy (e.g., hiking, biking, international travel, etc.), to infuse positive energy into my life and give me the perspective I need to move forward.

    I recognize that not everyone can take big chunks of time off. So, the next best thing is to make sure that you set aside time on a regular basis to reenergize and reflect. If you haven't read it already, there's a great HBR article, *Manage Your Energy Not Your Time*, that will help you determine how to recharge on a day-to-day basis.

    As for reflection time, even as little as fifteen to twenty minutes, periodically, can really help. I know that one size does not fit all, so figure out how often you should set aside time to stay in tune with your passion and priorities. When you do take the time, ask yourself the following questions:

    *   What do I enjoy most about what I do?
    *   What do I like the least?
    *   What am I tolerating (i.e., what is weighing me down)?
    *   What one step can I take to get more out of what I'm doing today?
    *   What one step can I take to move towards more of what I want?

I know that there are so many questions you could ask yourself, but these will get you started.

2. Surround yourself with the right people.

Energy, both positive and negative, is contagious. Surrounding yourself with people who can give you the support you need (whatever "support" looks like for you) and who get excited about the possibilities for you, can make a huge difference. Naysayers certainly have their value (e.g., they can help you think through potential risks) but they can also zap your energy, especially when you are trying to make a big, difficult change.

So take a look at who you interact with regularly or go to for advice, and think about the type of energy you get from each of them. You may realize that you need to make some shifts.

3. Make sure others understand your passion and skills.

Finally, always keep the pulse on what you are known for—your personal brand. If you don't know what it is today, you don't really know whether it's hurting or helping you. So, clarify what your brand is and what you want it to be.

Remember that when that perfect opportunity comes along, you want the key influencers and decision makers to think of *you*. If there is a big disconnect between what that perfect job entails, and what others consider your skills and passion, you probably won't get the job. So, set aside even five minutes each week to ensure that the right people understand the value you bring. I present on this topic all the time, so trust me when I say that you can do it tastefully and in a way that serves you and your company.

Let me end this article with a Call to Action. Determine one step you'll take to keep your passion front and center. Remember that small steps can lead to big results.

CONNECTING THE DOTS FOR OTHERS

I had a coaching call with my executive coach to talk about my Leadership System, and the steps I take my clients through to get breakthrough results. During the course of our conversation, I realized that there's one area that I *always* work on with my clients that they *never* realize they need to work on. It doesn't come up in our initial discussions about their coaching goals, *but it does affect their ability to truly lead with impact and build a strong leadership brand.*

Let me explain. Usually, when I ask a leader about the most critical things they want to accomplish from a business standpoint, they rattle off a list of things. The same thing happens when I ask about their teams. Very few of them can easily articulate the two or three areas of focus that guide everything they do.

For example, I have a client who has the remarkable ability to dive into a completely new area of responsibility, learn what she needs to, and restructure the work to maximize results. On top of that she empowers and develops her team to step up and sustain the performance. She has done this time and again, and can give me countless examples. Through our work together, she has come to realize that her primary focus is on *creating sustainable value while minimizing risk for the business and developing future leaders.* This is her beacon that guides everything she does.

By realizing this (i.e., Connecting the Dots for herself), she can now articulate a consistent message about her focus and intent. This provides tremendous value because she can give others a way to interpret what she says and does by constantly framing her actions and decisions in the context of her areas of focus.

Remember that others will draw conclusions about what you say and do using their own filters—and they may take away something different than you intend. Let me give you an example to further explain. I have another client (let's call her Michelle) who has a strong focus on supporting her team. This means that Michelle invests considerable time coaching her new hires, but she also recognizes the need to get her employees working independently without her day-to-day guidance.

So, she was surprised at her new hire's frustration when she scaled back her one-on-one time with him. Michelle knew that pulling back was the best support she could give him because it would serve him well in the long run. However, her employee didn't realize what she was doing. He didn't Connect the Dots in the same way Michelle thought he would. In fact, he had drawn the opposite conclusion. By explaining her primary focus, Michelle helped him understand that she *was* supporting him and how. He now has a way to interpret her actions and understand her expectations.

Remember that Connecting the Dots for others is not a "once and you're done" exercise. You have to do it again and again—and you can't do it unless you have Connected the Dots for yourself. So take advantage of the unique opportunity you have to provide a framework to give others insight into what you think is important, what success looks like, and what will guide your decisions. It will also create a stronger sense of conviction for you—about what you want to accomplish, how you will get there, and what you want to be known for as a leader.

ARE YOU MISSING THE TWO MOST IMPORTANT STEPS IN GIVING FEEDBACK?

Do you struggle with giving candid, constructive feedback? Read on if you answered, "Yes."

If you're like most managers and leaders, you have the best intentions when you are giving feedback. You want to communicate clearly and constructively without damaging the relationship, ultimately improving performance. As you know, this can be easier said than done.

So, as a feedback provider, what can you do to set up the conversation for success? Well, as I've coached people over the years, I have noticed two areas that can make a big difference:

1. **Describe what you observed.**

   When you are giving feedback, be sure to state the behavior you observed *in objective terms*. In other words, state the facts without interpreting them. This will make the person much more open to what you have to say and more likely to hear your underlying message.

   Let's use Jane as an example. From the past two team meetings you have attended you might think that Jane can't control her temper when others don't agree with her point of view. If you share your conclusion with her, it could immediately raise her defenses, resulting in a counterproductive argument.

   Instead, focus on the sharing the facts without sharing your interpretation. For example, you could say, "In the past two team meetings, you raised your voice at Jim and Sue when they disagreed with your suggestions."

2. **Communicate the impact of the behavior.**

   Sometimes you can focus so much on communicating the behavior that you may overlook the importance of explaining its impact. So, challenge yourself to think about any quantitative or qualitative consequences, and come up with at least two or three to share. This will go a long way in reinforcing the importance of the feedback, and will offer clues about what may be required to resolve the situation at hand.

Building on Jane's situation above, here are some examples: "Jim is embarrassed and does not want to attend future team meetings." "Sue has concerns about working with you." "The rest of the team does not want to bring up any ideas that you may disagree with." "Other leaders have heard about these two meetings, and are questioning your management style."

Although there are many other important steps involved in preparing to give feedback, I would encourage you to spend more time on these two. It can be the difference between a constructive and counterproductive conversation.

LEARNING THE UNWRITTEN RULES

I presented at the 11th Annual Diversity Summit in Houston on Negotiating for What You Want. At the conference, I heard a senior director from Catalyst (a leading organization focused on advancing women) speak about *Unwritten Rules: What You Don't Know Can Hurt You.* Like the presenter, I wish I could say that doing a good job is enough. It simply isn't. Although performance matters, understanding and playing by the unwritten rules can have a huge impact on your career advancement.

So I want to share just three of the strategies or "learning approaches" that Catalyst found in their research to help discover the unwritten rules. Their research goes on to share the effectiveness of each strategy in career advancement, and breaks down the data by gender.

1. **Observation**

   This approach involves taking time to really understand how thing work by paying attention to what other successful employees do, how they behave, and who gets promoted. Almost 90 percent of survey respondents said they had learned through observation, and 49 percent would recommend this approach.

   Most of us have a lot going on day-to-day, so this strategy may not get the attention it deserves. So, take a minute right now to ask yourself how often you take time to simply notice what is going on around you, and connect the dots. As organizations go through changes, and leaders move up or out, taking time to do this periodically may give you some important insight.

2. **Mentoring and Feedback**

   The second key learning approach centers around regularly seeking guidance and input from others about what it takes to succeed, staying in tune with your own behavior and performance, and using the information to understand what matters most in the organization. Eighty percent said they used this approach, and 32 percent would recommend it to others.

   Remember that engaging others in giving you guidance and feedback can also go a long way in creating sponsors, people who have a vested interested in your success and will advocate on your behalf.

3. Trial and Error

This strategy, which some may call "learning from the school of hard knocks," is all about figuring out what works and doesn't as you go along. Although a huge percentage of respondents learned unwritten rules this way—78 percent to be exact—only 18 percent found this approach helpful.

Wow, wouldn't it be nice if someone just saved you the trouble and handed you a list of all the unwritten rules? Since that probably won't happen, think about one small step you can take to put one of the most effective strategies into play for yourself.

WHEN SOMEONE PLAYS HARDBALL

I had a conversation with a talented leader who has achieved tremendous success in her career. She is currently in a tough political situation that has thrown her for a loop. A fellow leader at her company clearly wants to expand his span of responsibility and is blatantly playing hardball to make it happen. The situation has affected this woman's ability to stay level-headed, focused on what she needs to get done, and ultimately sustain her performance. And, because she carries her work frustration home, her personal life has suffered as well.

As someone who has worked with many large companies across industries, I have seen ugly politics time and again—and have personally experienced them myself. It's never fun, but you can navigate through it. So, here are three ideas that can help you:

1. **Identify your triggers.**

   We all have "buttons" and some know how to push them better than others. Yes, you know what I'm talking about. It could be a person who comes across as self-serving (e.g., blatantly schmoozing, taking all the credit, etc.) or does something equally frustrating.

   When you have a strong reaction (i.e., one that you keep replaying in your head or can't let go of), you need to identify what triggered it for you. *Usually it's not just about what that person said or did. Rather, at the core it has to do with something that you really value, that has been violated.*

   Sometimes it's hard to figure this one out by yourself because your emotions can cloud your judgment and ability to work through it. So, you may need to talk to a coach, colleague or confidant who can help you get to the heart of what's going on.

2. **Leverage the "Power of the Pause."**

   If nothing else, the next time you let yourself get triggered by this person just pause. *Remember that no one can make you feel or react a certain way unless you let them. Do you really want to give them that much power over you?* To some of you, my comments may sounds counterintuitive because you may want to blame the other person for the whole situation—"Of course it's their fault that I'm so stressed and frustrated!"

Do not underestimate the power you have. You know that you cannot control the other person, but you can control yourself—with deliberate focus and practice. I fully recognize this is much easier said than done, which is why people often need help to make the shift.

So start by taking a small step. Practice pausing when you get triggered. Even 2-3 seconds can give you just enough time to choose a different response.

3. Make a different choice.

Ok, this last step may sound like a statement of the obvious, but I can't tell you how much value people get from seeing it in black and white or hearing it. *Doing more of the same will never get you a different result. Period!*

The person who triggers your frustration can probably predict how you're going to respond. So, once you can make yourself pause, you will start to notice that you can make a different choice in the moment.

By choosing a different response, you can break the unproductive cycle. This will help you focus much more on what will serve you best in that situation and less on reacting to the other person's behavior.

So, let me end this article with a couple of final thoughts. First, don't underestimate what you can do in tough political situations to drive the outcome you want. Second, leverage the power *you* have when someone plays hardball. If nothing else, identify your triggers in the situation because doing that will help you get to a better outcome faster.

DO YOU HAVE MENTORS OR SPONSORS?

Whether you're a man or a woman, you've probably heard time and again how it important it is to have at least one strong mentor to guide you and help you develop the skills necessary to get to the next level in your career. Most large companies even offer formal or informal mentoring programs to both men and women. So, you might think that both genders benefit equally from having a mentor. However, a recent Harvard Business Review article, *Why Men Get More Promotions than Women*, highlights that men benefit more than women.

The article shares research from a 2010 study done by Catalyst, a leading nonprofit organization that works with businesses to build inclusive workplaces and expand opportunities for women and business. Here is one of the most notable findings from their research:

> *"Although women are mentored, they're not being promoted. A Catalyst study of more than 4,000 high potentials shows that more women than men have mentors—yet women are less likely to advance in their careers. That's because they're not actively sponsored the way the men are. Sponsors go beyond giving feedback and advice; they advocate for their mentees and help them gain visibility in the company. They fight to get their protégés to the next level."*

The article goes on to say that men and women both mention receiving valuable career advice from their mentors, but men predominantly describe being sponsored. Women explain that their mentoring relationships help them better understand themselves and how they work, and what they might need to change as they move up the corporate ladder. Men, on the other hand, tell more stories about how their bosses and mentors have helped them strategically plan their career moves, assume responsibility and leadership in new roles, and openly support their authority.

The research certainly has implications for organizations as they design mentoring programs and explore how to best support the advancement of women. But there are also important implications for what you should personally do. So, here are three suggestions to think about:

1. **Recognize the distinction between mentorship and sponsorship.**

   Both mentors and sponsors offer tremendous value in helping you determine how to develop yourself and proactively manage your career. Mentors typically serve as role models, providing guidance and perspective to help you further develop your skills, and navigate challenging political situations. Sponsors, on the other hand, give you exposure to opportunities and visibility to influential leaders, and advocate on your behalf.

2. **Have mentors and sponsors in your network.**

   Recognize that the skills required to be an effective mentor may be different from what it takes to be an effective sponsor. Mentors can typically hold any position in the organization and can help you close gaps in your skills, while sponsors have clout and yield considerable influence on key decision makers. So, remember to have both mentors and sponsors in your network, using your career goals as important context for who you engage.

3. **Be mindful of who you choose.**

   It may be more comfortable for you to choose individuals who look like you. In fact, the research shows that men tend to gravitate toward men and women to women. However when it comes to sponsors, more important than gender is the person's role and level in the organization. Remember that it's critical to gain sponsorship from leaders who hold senior level positions and have influence and power. As you think about mentors, think about the skills you are trying to build and who may be able to help you fill those gaps.

So, to get you started, take a look at your existing network in the context of what you're trying to accomplish personally and professionally. This will serve as an important guide to identify who to engage as mentors and sponsors to get the support you need.

FIVE PRACTICES OF EXEMPLARY LEADERS

I had the privilege of attending a workshop led by Jim Kouzes, the co-author of *The Leadership Challenge*. For those of you who have not heard of this book, you should take a look. Based on over 30 years of research, he and Barry Posner identified five common practices of leaders who make extraordinary things happen.

Before we review the five practices, let's first define leadership. Kouzes & Posner define a leader as someone whose direction you would *willingly follow*. In other words, you can't be a leader without followers. To further define leadership the authors asked, "What do you look for and admire in a leader?" Here are the top four attributes and the percentage of respondents who mentioned them:

1. Honest (85%)
2. Forward looking (70%)
3. Inspiring (69%)
4. Competent (64%)

Over the 30 years that they have asked this question, the authors have consistently gotten *the same top four responses in the same order*. When you look at these four items collectively, they underscore the importance of credibility when it comes to leadership.

So, now let's take a look at the Five Practices of Exemplary Leaders.

1. Model the way.

This practice is about establishing principles and standards for how people should be treated, and how goals should be pursued. As a leader, you must first clarify what *you* believe in and what you're willing to take a stand for before you can articulate it to others. Then you need to align your actions with what you believe in (i.e., do what you say you will do).

2. Inspire a shared vision

Through their research, Kouzes & Posner note that what distinguishes leaders from colleagues is their ability to be forward looking. Leaders can envision the future and create a compelling image of what the organization can become—and they truly believe that they can make a difference.

Contrary to what you may think, a leader does not have to originate the vision of the future. In fact, leaders may develop their vision by carefully tuning into what they hear from others. No matter where the vision comes from, the leader must be able to help others see it, engage them in it, and help them understand how they fit into it.

3. Challenge the process.

As you might expect, leadership is not about maintaining the status quo. Leaders Challenge the Process by experimenting, taking risks, and accepting disappointments as valuable learning opportunities. On a weekly basis, you can keep this exemplary practice at the forefront by asking, "What have I done this week to improve so that I'm more effective than I was last week?"

4. Enable others to act.

At the core of Enabling Others to Act is mutual respect and trust. Leaders understand that this can sustain extraordinary efforts, so they strive to create a trusting environment and take time to develop others.

In the workshop, Jim Kouzes challenged each of us to ask ourselves before every interaction with every person in our organizations, "What can I do in this interaction to make sure this person feels more capable as a result of what I say and do?" I would challenge you to do the same.

5. Encourage the heart.

The last practice is Encourage the Heart. Research shows that the highest performing leaders are more open and caring, express more affection, demonstrate more passion, and are more positive, grateful and encouraging than lower performers. Knowing that achieving extraordinary results takes hard work, strong leaders understand the power of recognizing and celebrating how others are making a difference.

Now that you've read about each exemplary practice, identify which ones you already do well and choose one practice to emphasize further. Remember that these practices don't have to be time consuming—it's all about taking small steps that lead you to big results. So, I urge you to choose a small step to implement from this list below or identify one of your own:

- Think about when you performed at your best as a leader. What did you do in that situation that you can leverage today (you may have used several Exemplary Practices)?

- Take five minutes to talk to your team about exciting possibilities you see for the future (Inspire a Shared Vision).

- Ask, "What have I done this week to improve, so that I'm more effective than last week?" (Challenge the Process)

- Ask, "What can I do during this interaction to make sure this person feels more capable as a result of what I say and do?" (Enable Others to Act)

- Ask, "What can I do this week to encourage my team, so that they perform at a higher level?" (Encourage the Heart)

THE FINE ART OF INFLUENCE

Influence has so many implications, from getting your ideas heard to getting the support and resources you need to implement them. For some the fine art of influence comes naturally, but for most it requires concerted effort. Let's start by taking a look at a common definition of influence.

> *Influence is the capacity or power of persons or things to be a compelling force on or produce effects on the actions, behavior, opinions, etc., of others. (Source: dictionary.com)*

Well, who wouldn't want to be a compelling force that affects what others think or do?! Some of you might be thinking that this sounds more like manipulating others to get what you want. However, what I'm referring to is learning how to develop win/win scenarios that allow you to get traction by being authentic, considering what is important to others, and doing what's right for your company.

For example, I have a client who is trying to take the performance of her organization to the next level but keeps getting tangled in a web of politics. She needs help from another group to get the results she wants, but hasn't been able to influence them to collaborate. Her focus is not self-serving. She truly has the organization's best interest in mind.

So, we zeroed in on one critical relationship that could influence my client's results dramatically. Below is a list of questions that I asked her in the context of influencing a specific person to take action. These questions may help you the next time you want to exert more influence.

What are you really trying to accomplish?

First, be clear about what you want and why. It will help you better understand and communicate your underlying intent. For example, you may want someone to invite you to a specific leadership team meeting. On the surface, to them it might seem that you just want to schmooze, but in reality you have and want to share key information with the group so that they can make better business decisions. Clarifying and sharing your intent will lead you to make the request in a way that will help the other person understand the "so what."

How are you perceived by the other person?

Your credibility and reputation impacts whether the other person notices or really hears what you want. So, take time to reflect about what the other person thinks of you and how their "filter" might affect what they think of your request.

In my client's case, the other person thinks of her as smart, direct, and focused on doing the right thing. However, they don't know each other well, so my client may need to reinforce some of those attributes in her communication.

What is important to the other person?

Asking this question will help you zero in on what motivates the other person. It could range from looking good to their boss, to wanting to get promoted, to achieving a specific goal, or working less. The possibilities are endless. If you don't know the answer to this question, talk to others who might.

Where is the common ground for you both?

This final step brings it all together by combining your intent with what matters to the other person. People tend to be much more receptive if they view your request as aligned with their goals and objectives. So, think about how you can frame your request or what you want in this context.

By taking even a couple of minutes to think through these questions, you can dramatically shift how you frame an idea or make a request—and your influence on the outcome. It can be the difference between sounding nitpicky and self-serving versus focused on something that matters to you and the other person involved, and that brings value to the organization. Give it a shot and see what happens.

SETTING YOURSELF UP FOR SUCCESS
IN A NEGOTIATION

I presented at the Women's Global Leadership Conference in Energy & Technology in Houston. The topic was How to successfully negotiate for a raise—*How to get past your dread, develop a win/win approach, and negotiate for what you want.*

In this article, I have broadened my comments from what I presented there to apply to a variety of career situations—where you might be negotiating a pay raise, a high profile assignment or key role, or for something else you really want.

There are tons of articles about negotiating and the best way to approach it. So, rather than try to cover all that territory, I want to share two things that are mentioned less often but have a huge impact on your success.

1. Create the right perception.

One of the things I coach and do workshops on is Getting the Visibility You Want, which is all about *strategically* informing others and giving more visibility to your skills and contributions. Take some time to think about who needs to understand how you are adding value and who will influence the ultimate decision about whether to give you what you are asking for. If you don't know already, find out what their perception of your performance is today and where you may need to close some gaps.

Let me be clear, this is *not* about creating a false image. It is about proactively helping others understand your value and helping them understand how to best leverage your skills and talent. We all know this doesn't happen overnight, so allow enough time to close any gaps in perception.

Also, remember that how you "show up" in the conversation where you ask for what you want matters. So, think about how you want to be viewed or perceived in the negotiation. For example you might want to be seen as confident, reasonable, committed to the company's success, and looking for a win/win for you and the company. Whatever it may be, think about how to frame up the conversation to reinforce that image.

2. Understand how you will get in your own way.

Many of us have fears or anxiety about negotiating or asking for what we want. So, think about how you might get in your own way in advance. It could be a belief or concern that keeps you from asking for what you want. For example, I have a client who was really concerned that she would be viewed as greedy because she was already paid well, even though the data showed that she was clearly underpaid relative to others at her level.

Another client who was asking for a nontraditional role feared the worst, that they would just say, "We can't give you what you want. Just leave if you're not happy." Test these beliefs by looking for confirming and disconfirming evidence. More often than not, our own fears are the biggest barrier to getting what we want.

In both of the examples above, I worked with my clients to identify their mental roadblocks and how they might react in the face of resistance, and develop strategies to keep both from getting in their way. I am excited to say that both of my clients got *everything* they asked for.

There are so many things I could have covered in this article, and so much I still want to share with you. For now, think about how you can start applying these two concepts, whether you are asking for something big or small

IS THE GLASS REALLY HALF EMPTY?

If you're like most people, you've been in situations that haven't turned out like you wanted or expected. For example, you might have been passed up for an exciting opportunity or promotion that you felt well-qualified for, or you didn't get the pay increase you were expecting. We've all been faced with disappointment in one way or another in our personal and professional lives.

The question is, "How can you work through it in a positive way?" In my work with high performing leaders and in my own life, I have found the work of Martin Seligman, the acclaimed author of *Learned Optimism*, to be extremely helpful. He offers a simple model called "ABCDE," which helps you recognize and dispute pessimistic thoughts and replace them with optimism and hope. Once you recognize that you have a pessimistic thought that seems unwarranted, argue against it using the ABCDE model.

A stands for **adversity**
B for the **beliefs** you automatically have when it occurs
C for the usual **consequences** of your routine belief
D for the **disputation** of your routine belief
E for the **energization** you get when you dispute it successfully

Here's an example to bring it to life.

Adversity: I didn't get the promotion I had worked so hard for all year long.

Beliefs: My boss doesn't value what I have to offer. He still thinks I'm not experienced enough. What am I still doing here?

Consequences: I'm really disappointed and am not sure I can continue to work somewhere that I'm not appreciated and don't have a future. I'm so tired of the political games at this company.

Disputation: Maybe I'm overlooking some important facts. No one else at my level got promoted this year. In fact, several people were laid off. My boss gave me good feedback on my performance and I did get a good pay increase. He explained what a financially challenging year it has been for the company. I don't think I specifically told him that I expected a promotion this year.

Energization: I *am* getting recognition for my work when I really think about it—it's just in a different way than I expected. I need to follow up with my boss to have an open conversation with him about the promotion I want, and how and when we can make it happen.

I encourage you to try out this model for the adverse events that you face—whether personal or professional, major or minor. ***One of the most powerful aspects of the model is that it forces you to look for evidence to dispute your negative beliefs.*** You may be surprised at the energy you get as you succeed in overcoming them.

LESSONS FROM HALL OF FAMERS
AIKMAN AND STAUBACH

I heard Roger Staubach and Troy Aikman speak in an intimate setting at a United Way Tocqueville event. As a young girl relocating from England to Texas in the late 1970's, I became a huge Dallas Cowboys fan. So, it was exciting to hear personal stories from two people that I admire and respect.

Scott Murray moderated the discussion, asking Troy and Roger what shaped their careers, who has had the biggest impact on them, and what led them to get engaged in the community. As I listened to them speak, there were three things that really jumped out at me, and they may serve as important reminders for you:

1. **Be open to the possibilities.**

   When asked whether they thought they would ever play football professionally, let alone be quarterbacks, Troy and Roger both said no. Troy said that he knew from a very young age that he wanted to be a professional athlete, but like Roger his passion was baseball.

   Roger talked about how his coach saw potential in him and encouraged him to try out for quarterback. When Roger resisted and asked, "Why do you think I'd make a good quarterback?" his coach explained that the other players always listened to him. His coach recognized Roger's innate leadership ability.

   In Roger's story, it was clear that his coach's interest and guidance led him down a path he would never have chosen for himself. But Roger was open to the possibilities and was willing to take a chance. His choice is what ultimately made a difference—and the payoff was huge.

2. **One person can make a huge difference.**

   When asked who has influenced him the most, Troy spoke from the heart about his mother. As an adult and parent, he now fully recognizes her sacrifices, her commitment to his rigorous schedule of practices and games, and her support throughout the years. This in turn has shaped his relationship with his daughters and increased his desire to make a difference in the lives of others.

As you know, there are many small ways that you can show your support each day—whether it's taking five minutes to lend an ear, share your wisdom, or acknowledge what you appreciate about someone. If you have ever been on the receiving end of this, you know it can have a huge impact for a small investment of time. What will you do this week to acknowledge that person who has most influenced you?

3. **Remember to pay it forward.**

   Troy and Roger are prime examples of people who have put their celebrity to good use, to give back and affect change in their communities. Troy Aikman co-chairs the Healthy Zone Schools community initiative to reduce childhood obesity and he and Roger are both major philanthropists.

   As you think about yourself, what legacy do you want to leave? Who could benefit from your natural talents, skills and passion? Could it be the person next to your office struggling with a tough issue at work, a teenager who needs guidance and direction, or someone else right under your nose? Take time to notice others around you and use your wisdom and experience to help them.

Although you may not be a Hall of Famer like Troy Aikman or Roger Staubach, you do have the power of choice—in how you allow others to challenge you and take you in directions you never imagined, and in how you "bring others up." So, I want to challenge you to take one small step in one of the three areas above. You know I'm a firm believer that small steps can lead to big results.

ABOUT THE AUTHOR

Neena Newberry leapt into entrepreneurship in 2008 by launching Newberry Executive Solutions to focus on her passion for developing strong leaders, especially women. She left a more than 16-year consulting and human resources career, and a role leading performance management and career planning for 34,000 employees on Deloitte's U.S. HR Executive Team. She didn't know the economy would tank just three months later, teaching her lessons that would benefit her clients.

Grounded in practical business experience, Neena develops leaders through Purpose, Presence, and Power. The result: rave reviews about her company's products and services from *Fortune* 500 clients such as AT&T, Marriott, PepsiCo, Shell, and Sysco, and organizations like the United Way and the George W. Bush Presidential Center. Not to mention Neena's chapter in the *MBA Women's Guide to Success,* the *WOW! Women On the Way to Peak Performance Program*[SM], and this book, *Show Up. Step Up. Step Out.*

Newberry's credentials include more than 20 years of advising and coaching business leaders, an MBA, a Professional in Human Resources Certification, and a Professional Certified Coach credential from the International Coach Federation.

Through volunteer work with Collaborative for Children in Houston and the United Way of Metropolitan Dallas (UWMD), Newberry has been a long-term champion of education reform. Her other endeavors include an adjunct professorship in executive education at the SMU Cox School of Business; vice president of the board of the National Association of Women MBAs; global and local leadership roles with the International Coach Federation; chair of the UMWD Advocacy Committee; and author of leadership articles for her alma mater, the McCombs School of Business at the University of Texas at Austin.

Neena has designed a life that allows her to spend quality time with her family while pursuing her passion. She just broke in her first glove learning to play baseball with her son, who keeps her grounded and energized. Neena's sense of adventure takes her outdoors, most recently hiking 50 miles over five days at the Grand Canyon.

9809192R00082

Made in the USA
San Bernardino, CA
27 March 2014